CONTENTS

INTRODUCTION

Are YOU RUNNING your life or is your life running you? Do you increasingly feel at the mercy of inner and outer conflicts that you believe are beyond your understanding or control? Whether you are aware of it or not, the various pressures imposed by your home and work environments take a daily toll on your physical and emotional well-being. When these are accompanied by low self-esteem, avoiding difficulties, or denial that there are any problems, the consequences can be very damaging to your relationships, to work, and, most importantly, to yourself. Your distress or discomfort may not just manifest itself in feelings of victimization and powerlessness, however—unwanted habits and addictions are also a strong signal to yourself and others that all is not well.

Taking control of your life means deciding that you are going to be the "driver" and not simply a "passenger," and taking full responsibility for the direction your life takes, reprogramming your attitudes positively.

It's a jungle out there
Like an untended garden, there may be negative parts of your life that have grown out of control for lack of care and attention.

What is control?

Life is full of unpredictable events, and, inevitably, there will be times when you feel overwhelmed, faced with situations you feel unable to make sense of or resolve. To have control over your life is to understand yourself—what makes you tick—and be willing to work on those aspects of yourself that are causing you difficulties. It also involves developing a confident, assertive response to change, viewing it as an integral part of life that doesn't simply cause upheaval, but offers opportunities for creative decisions and growth.

Take Carol. When her father died, Renee, her invalid mother, insisted on moving into Carol's home to be taken care of, despite the fact that Carol had two small children to look after. Carol's husband, Fred, resented Renee's presence in the household and started to make increasing demands on Carol's time. Carol felt desperate, slipping into a victim mentality where life seemed loaded against her. Once she saw how her negative feelings were making her seriously depressed, she reprogrammed them so that she could view the situation calmly and rationally. She acknowledged the powerful emotional pull her mother had over her, and at the same time realized that she could not be all things to all people. Eventually she persuaded Renee to move out into nearby sheltered accommodation, where she could visit her regularly.

Even people who seem to have an enviable degree of control can feel defeated by certain situations. Sara, for instance, was an efficient manager

Take Control of Your Life

TIME LIFE BOOKS

MINDPOWER
JOURNEY THROUGH THE MIND AND BODY
COOKERY AROUND THE WORLD
LOST CIVILIZATIONS
THE ILLUSTRATED LIBRARY OF THE EARTH
SYSTEM EARTH
LIBRARY OF CURIOUS AND UNUSUAL FACTS
BUILDING BLOCKS
A CHILD'S FIRST LIBRARY OF LEARNING
VOYAGE THROUGH THE UNIVERSE
THE THIRD REICH
MYSTERIES OF THE UNKNOWN
TIME-LIFE HISTORY OF THE WORLD
FITNESS, HEALTH & NUTRITION
HEALTHY HOME COOKING
UNDERSTANDING COMPUTERS
THE ENCHANTED WORLD
LIBRARY OF NATIONS
PLANET EARTH
THE GOOD COOK
THE WORLD'S WILD PLACES

MINDPOWER

Take Control of Your Life

TIME-LIFE BOOKS
Amsterdam

MINDPOWER

Created, edited, and designed by DK Direct Limited,
62-65 Chandos Place, London WC2N 4HS

A DORLING KINDERSLEY BOOK

DK DIRECT LIMITED
Series Editor Luci Collings
Deputy Series Editor Sue Leonard
Senior Editor Jennifer Jones
Editors Fran Baines, Sue George, Kate Swainson

Managing Art Editor Ruth Shane
Designers Sue Caws, Jamie Hanson

Publisher Jonathan Reed
Editorial Director Reg Grant
Design Director Ed Day
Production Manager Ian Paton
Editorial Consultant Keren Smedley

Contributors Vida Adamoli, Terry Burrows, Julia Cole, Victoria Davenport, Ann Kay,
Joseph O'Connor, Dennis Sartain, Ruth Shane, Patricia Spungin-Cook, Sue Temple

Editorial Researcher L. Brooke
Picture Researcher Sharon Southren
Indexer Ella Skene

TIME-LIFE BOOKS EUROPEAN EDITION
Staff for Take Control of Your Life
Editorial Manager Christine Noble
Editorial Assistant Mark Stephenson
Design Director Mary Staples
Designer Dawn McGinn
Editorial Production Justina Cox
European edition edited by Tim Cooke

First Time-Life European English language edition 1996
ISBN 0 7054 1632 1
TIME-LIFE is a trademark of Time-Warner Inc., U.S.A.

Printed by GEA, Milan, and bound by GEP, Cremona, Italy

of a clothing store who devised five-year plans, made detailed lists of appointments and dates, then went to pieces when there was a minor problem at home. Once she learned to view her life as a whole, and take control in all areas—both at work and at home—she felt much better, and less inclined to hide her fear of tackling personal issues by hiding behind super-efficiency at work.

"Know thyself"

This wise dictum, found in the temple of Delphi, is as relevant to us today as it was to the people of ancient Greece. Understanding who you are and what you want is key to taking control of your life.

From our fingerprints to our thought processes, each one of us is a unique creation, although behavioral research shows that people fall into two general categories. In their book, *Relax, Dealing with Stress*, authors Watts and Cooper call these categories Internals and Externals, and show how much parental influence affects our ability to direct our lives as adults.

• Internals are people who see themselves as having control over events and the choices that they make. An Internal is likely to have come from a background that valued individuality, encouraged a healthy degree of risk-taking and experimentation, viewed change with curiosity and excitement, and taught how to approach disappointment in a constructive way. As a result, Internals learn to trust their talents, judgment, and ideas. Crucially, they form the conviction that their life will be what they decide to make of it.

• Externals, on the other hand, tend to feel that their lives are decided by other people and circumstances outside themselves. They will have received less positive influences during their development. They might have been subjected to constant criticism, or surrounded by an atmosphere that expected failure.

Flexibility

There will always be times when you feel that your coping skills are being overstretched. Part of taking control is to recognize this and to use your awareness to build a robust flexibility that allows you to recover from setbacks and move on.

In this volume, we offer strategies for getting back on top of things, skills that can be used in a wide variety of situations. They are strategies of empowerment—designed to free you to exert a positive influence in all areas of your life, and to gain a truly positive sense of self.

GET IN CONTROL

Few people feel that everything in their life is out of control all of the time. One issue that we mentioned on pages 6 and 7 is that of feeling confident in some areas of our lives, but not in others. For example, you might be an excellent boss when it comes to meeting productivity and financial targets, but flounder when you have to discuss a personal issue with an employee. Or human situations may pose no problem, but your work life is dogged by a sense of inadequacy—such as the woman who has successfully brought up a young family but is suddenly beset by doubts on returning to work.

You can't always control events and other people —neither should you try to. What you can do, however, is control yourself and your reactions. One way to start is by looking at those situations that make you feel in control and good about yourself and those that produce the opposite effect. Remember that the choice to live with confidence, optimism, and courage is yours. All these qualities can be developed—and they can steer you toward positive, and not negative, control.

Negative control

Negative control is the need to control people or events outside yourself, or to get others to do things for you. Whereas positive control is rooted in mastery of yourself, negative control often seeks to impose discipline on people or things that lie outside— even to the extent of wanting them to control you.

Negative control is usually driven by fear. Lynn was 40 when she discovered that her husband Dan was having an affair. Despite the fact that the marriage had been unhappy for years, the thought of coping on her own filled Lynn with dread. Feeling trapped and helpless, Lynn focused all her energy on controlling her home: she became fanatically tidy. If anyone so much as displaced a cushion, she became disproportionately agitated. Too frightened to deal with the real issues of her life, she clung desperately to controlling its insignificant details.

Fear and feeling out of control are keys to all kinds of obsessive behavior. In compulsive hand-washing, for example, or the irrational need to check and recheck locks, people act out the compulsion to give them an illusion of control over their anxiety.

Addicts are living out another form of negative control. While he was "high," Tom forgot his problems and so escaped from having to face them. His "control" consisted of creating an existence centred around procuring and taking drugs—within this little world, he felt totally in control.

Fear of the uncertainties of life can also lead to an over-dependence on another person. Co-dependency—where two people foster and become reliant on each other's inadequacies—is something that relationship counselors see again and again. It seems that this is also related to a failure to take control of your own life, since it creates a self-perpetuating state of powerlessness and loss of independence in both partners.

Positive control

When Lynn's husband finally left, her first reaction was one of panic. It was not until she sought help from a therapist that she found the courage to go back to work at the bank where she had worked many years before, and was able to begin the slow process of rebuilding her self-esteem.

Lynn came to see that she had never taken full responsibility for her life and had blamed her husband for the failure of their relationship. She had let him direct the course of things, and had then resented him for it. In order to feel in control, she had used various manipulative tactics to win what she felt were small triumphs over her husband, such as persuading him to go on foreign holidays although he hated going abroad.

For Lynn, the determination to take charge of her own happiness and fulfillment was an essential step in assuming control of her life. Soon she was coping with the children, the house and garden, and her job, and the effort and perseverance that all of this demanded strengthened her inner resolve and showed her what she was capable of. As her view of herself as helpless diminished, so did her fanatical tidiness, and she became more relaxed about small, unimportant details.

By accessing your strengths and using them, you can establish an outlook that is both positive and dynamic. Make things happen rather than waiting passively to see what "Fate" delivers to your door, and you will discover the real meaning of freedom.

In full bloom
Run your life like a well-kept garden and any weeds of self-doubt and negativity will be easy to spot and control.

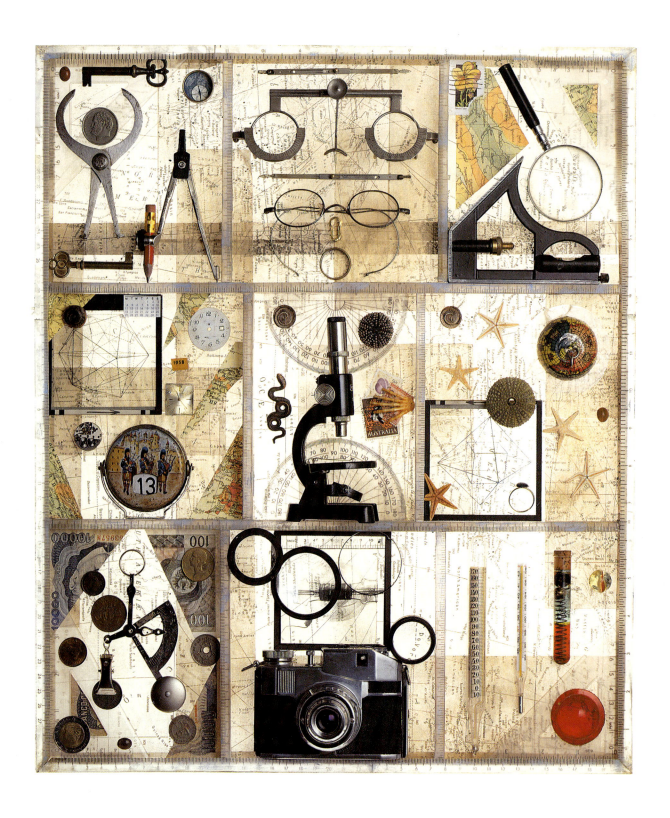

CHAPTER ONE

VALUES, ATTITUDES, AND BELIEFS

YOUR VALUES, ATTITUDES, and beliefs are what give meaning and direction to your life. When you live in harmony with them, all tends to be well. But if you are not aware of your bedrock values, you may unwittingly find yourself living at odds with them. You may also hold attitudes and beliefs that work against rather than for you. This chapter encourages you to get to know yourself better: what drives you, where you want to go, and what makes life worth living.

We invite you first to take a closer look at your values, attitudes, and beliefs—what they are, and where they may have come from. How accurately does your outer life reflect these inner qualities? Are you holding on to any out-dated or negative attitudes and beliefs that could be usefully revised, or even jettisoned? These ideas are explored further in the quiz "Check Your Attitudes" on pages 14-15, and "Identify the False Belief" on pages 16-17.

Just as important is the direction your life is taking. Do you find yourself habitually drifting, half hoping things will work out somehow? "Knowing What You Want" (pp. 20-21), and having clear, realistic goals are the keys to a fulfilling and enriched life. Part of this process also involves knowing what you enjoy and making sure you include more of these activities in your life—you will find the quiz "Measure Your Pleasure Level" on pages 22-23 useful here.

However, it's hard to make the most of your life if you are suffering from stress—a problem that's endemic in modern society. We examine the causes of stress, and how to minimize its effects.

Another area that often causes difficulties in our lives is the hidden triggers that make us behave in ways we don't understand—these triggers stem from early childhood experiences, and left unresolved can have serious repercussions in our adult lives. It's also important to know how you experience the world and, even more crucially, how you might control your reactions to those experiences—here we consider some of the techniques developed by practioners of Neuro-Linguistic Programming.

Finally, we look at the fears and doubts that hold us back in life. The quiz "Are You Holding Back?" on pages 34-35 is followed by advice on how to face your fears and ways to challenge them. In a similar vein, we also consider those times when you may feel you are a victim, and how to assert yourself.

KNOWING YOURSELF IS THE KEY TO A HAPPIER, MORE FULFILLING LIFE—
ONCE YOU KNOW WHAT DRIVES YOU, AND WHERE YOU WANT TO GO, YOU
WILL HAVE THE CLARITY AND COMMITMENT TO REACH YOUR GOALS.

WHAT MAKES YOU TICK?

VALUES, ATTITUDES, AND BELIEFS color the way people see the world—and can have a positive or a negative effect on their behavior. This doesn't only apply to individuals: whole communities and nations also adopt behavioral patterns based on these powerful influences. Values, attitudes, and beliefs can be so deep-seated that people may be unaware of the effect that they are having on their lives. So, examining your values, attitudes, and beliefs will uncover some essential truths about what makes you tick—and reveal which ones are working against you.

Check your values

A value is how you personally feel something *should* be—the way things would work in your ideal world. Your values form the bedrock of your life, providing overall guidelines and offering hints as to what you consider to be meaningful. When someone says that he or she is making a "value judgment," what they mean is that he or she is making a subjective comparison, placing one thing above another, according to his or her personal values.

Values come in different shapes and sizes, such as: "Everyone in the world should be treated equally, regardless of ethnic origin or gender;" "Personal happiness should always come before wealth;" and "Telling even a white lie is wrong—a lie is a lie." Some people are very aware of their values, and always live in harmony with them. But most are not always fully conscious of what they consider to be important and a clash of values can occur. For instance, you may have a well-paid, interesting job that you feel is important to your happiness, but promotes an idea or makes a product with which you disagree. If this happens it can leave you feeling unhappy or uncomfortable.

Cast a little light

Think of your values, attitudes, and beliefs as the different faces of a very precious jewel—your personal identity. Holding this jewel up for scrutiny and examining each face in turn will throw valuable light on what makes you tick and how you can change for the better.

Alter your attitudes

Attitudes can be defined in a number of ways, one of which is that an attitude is what you *feel* about something. Examples of attitudes are "I enjoy going to work," "No matter how old you are it should be possible to learn," and "Comedy programs on television are a waste of time." In each of these statements, there is an emotional dimension that colors the belief (see below)—and where the emotions are engaged, behavior tends to follow. This explains why people may say they believe one thing, yet their actions don't bear this out. For example, you may believe that smoking damages your health, but your attitude is "It won't affect me."

Many of our attitudes come from what is accepted by society. However, attitudes are also shaped by our temperament and personal history. Someone with a diffident, bookish temperament, for instance, may hold attitudes that are skeptical and questioning. An extroverted, dramatic person may well have vehement, even extreme, attitudes.

Challenge your beliefs

The terms attitudes and beliefs are often used interchangeably. However, although both attitudes and beliefs give rise to certain behavior, actions need not necessarily be part of a belief. Beliefs are strong convictions that can range from the factual—"I believe that eating fresh fruit and vegetables improves your health"—to the highly personal—"I believe that I can succeed in life."

We get our beliefs from many different sources. Parents and teachers are influential in our early years, but other people and significant events shape our beliefs in adult life. Beliefs can be altered by experience, and they can also be altered consciously, for we tend to base our beliefs on "evidence." You will often notice what confirms a particular belief, and discount evidence to the contrary.

Beliefs are very powerful: Positive beliefs support the idea that you can succeed; negative beliefs will tend to hold you back. Your beliefs are often rein-

forced by your attitudes. For example, if you generally believe people are untrustworthy, you will notice when they are, and generally be suspicious of them. They in turn may be wary of you because of your approach, thus reinforcing your belief. Beliefs give meaning to our experiences—and it is the significance that we attach to these experiences that shapes our lives, not what happens to us.

CHECK YOUR ATTITUDES

How do you react when faced with an awkward situation such as a disagreement or confrontation? Do you tend to blame someone else for the problem and always make your own needs paramount, or do you immediately let the other person's opinions and wishes take precedence? Try the following questionnaire to help you assess your attitudes in this area, then check your responses against the conclusions on pages 138-139.

1. Somebody asks to borrow some money that you really need for yourself. Do you:
a) State that the money is for your own use and explain to the other person why you feel that lending it would be inappropriate?
b) Simply lend the money, feeling disappointed that it will not be available for your own needs?
c) Lend the money, but make the other person fully aware of how much you have given up?
d) Deal with the request as a confrontation, expressing your anger at having been put into such a difficult position?

2. At short notice you have to make a presentation at work. Do you:
a) Use your experience and skills to prepare yourself, and your material, to the best of your ability?
b) Think that if the audience asks challenging questions you will show them that you know more than they do, despite your lack of preparation?
c) Assume that your audience knows much more than you do and won't be interested in anything that you might have to say?
d) Excuse the quality of your material because you were not given enough time to prepare?

3. You get home to find that everywhere is a huge mess. Do you:
a) Explain your feelings of annoyance and get everyone to help tidying up?
b) Tidy up yourself, thinking how inconsiderate your family is?
c) Shout and throw everything on the floor?
d) Mutter complaints, then resentfully sort out the mess, making sure everyone feels uncomfortable?

4. You are in a position where you have to ask someone for a favor. Do you:
a) Feel that if the person refuses it will be a sign he or she doesn't like you?
b) Believe that a refusal would be a personal attack, warranting an angry response?
c) Feel that your needs are important, but that the person has a right to refuse if he or she wants to?
d) Think that you couldn't possibly ask the person?

What shall I do?
Maybe you don't always pass the buck when faced with problems, but perhaps you still find it hard to decide what to do.

5. Someone whose opinion you respect criticizes you. Do you:

a) Immediately lose your temper, rejecting the person's right to criticize and reversing the criticism back onto him or her?

b) Listen to what is being said, acknowledging the elements that you judge to be valid?

c) Take it in without comment, allowing it to reinforce your own low opinion of yourself?

d) Attempt to justify yourself, making the other person feel that he or she is being unfair?

6. Your partner forgets your anniversary or birthday. Do you:

a) Feel upset, but resigned to the fact that you are not always uppermost in your partner's mind?

b) Sulk and do your best to make your partner feel as guilty and uncomfortable as possible?

c) Provoke an argument without accepting any explanation or apology that your partner offers?

d) Make your partner aware of the occasion and propose ways of celebrating?

7. You have taken your car to the garage for its usual routine service and the mechanic calls to say it needs yet more money spent on it. Do you:

a) Follow all the mechanic's recommendations, being sure that he or she knows best?

b) Get upset, saying that you can't afford it and may as well scrap your car?

c) Argue with the mechanic and accuse him or her of trying to cheat you, because you are sure the car is fine?

d) Tell him or her you would like to get another estimate for the work, and take whichever one is cheaper?

8. You are asked to do something you don't want to do. Do you:

a) Simply do it—against your wishes?

b) Explain in a reasonable way why you are not prepared to do what has been asked?

c) Do it unwillingly, letting the other person know how inconvenient it is, and what a large favor you are doing him or her?

d) Rebuke the person asking you, accusing him or her of being out of line?

9. You are in a face-to-face confrontation with someone. Do you:

a) Just give in?

b) Burst into tears?

c) Try to shout louder than your antagonist?

d) Attempt to understand the situation and deal with it?

10. You need to complain to a shop or return something you purchased. Do you:

a) State your request clearly, dealing firmly with any argument you encounter?

b) Shout and make a scene?

c) Blame inadequacies in the shop or staff for making it impossible for you to have chosen correctly?

d) Pad your complaint with apologies and excuses?

Change your attitudes

Once you've checked your scores on pages 138-139, you will have a clearer idea of how you tend to react. Accepting responsibility for your actions means that you will maintain your own self-respect and be able to command the respect of others. On the other hand, blaming other people usually increases hostility and puts them on the defensive. It is important for you to feel that you have the same rights as anyone else to express your wishes and let your needs be known; this is not the same as trying to make others do what you want.

Look at the problem
Dealing openly and assertively with difficult situations will promote your own self-esteem and that of others.

IDENTIFY THE FALSE BELIEF

Everyone has beliefs—ideas they think are true—about themselves and life in general. But while beliefs are often positive and supportive, they can also distort people's perceptions of life around them. Such mistaken beliefs can create a false view that prevents the person who holds them from fulfilling their true potential.

Limiting beliefs

False beliefs typically spring from exaggeration, generalization, and distortion. For example, "I'll fail my course," is an exaggeration that starts from a belief that has a degree of truth—"I find writing essays hard"—and takes it much too far. In generalization, one particular example is taken, wrongly, to represent all possibilities—"My train is late" may turn into the belief "Trains never arrive on time." Distortion, meanwhile, allows a person to ignore facts and examples, especially positive ones, that contradict whatever false beliefs he or she might have adopted. The belief "You can't rely on anyone" conveniently ignores the many people who provide essential services that are taken for granted, from nurses to airline pilots.

Look at the facts

The idea that "wrong" behavior follows on from "wrong" beliefs is illustrated by the following situation involving Peter, a sales representative for an office supplies company, and his manager, Jenny. When she gives him the task of visiting one of the company's small customers and finding out what they need, Jenny does not tell Peter that, although the company is small, it is in a position to give a good referral to another large client. She believes he does not need to know this, because it might make him nervous. Peter, however, is resentful. He believes that Jenny undervalues him and he always gets to deal with the unimportant clients. But he does not say anything, believing that Jenny might bear a grudge and damage his chances of promotion—both distortions.

Peter sees the client and, believing the visit to be trivial, does not give a good impression. The client does not give the referral and Jenny is annoyed, blaming Peter. In turn, he blames Jenny, "You should have told me the full facts!"

Odd one out
Any false, limiting belief that goes unrecognized and unchallenged will strike a discordant note. Once addressed and weeded out, harmony can be restored.

Both Peter and Jenny see the behavior rather than the belief, and make their judgments about the other based on that behavior. Jenny believes Peter is nervous with important clients, after she saw him acting awkwardly in a meeting last month. However, Peter was simply feeling unwell that day. Peter also holds distorted beliefs. Although he does see many small clients, he also sees important ones. But he disregards those occasions as unusual.

They do, however, share one false belief: that when things go wrong it must be someone's fault, instead of a shared miscommunication. Blaming one person implies that that person is totally responsible—a distortion of the truth. Honest, straightforward discussion between them would go a long way to solving their problems. But to establish a more effective working relationship they both need to identify and change their limiting beliefs.

Increasing communication

Jane and John have been married for five years. Jane is feeling neglected: John never tells her that he loves her any more and because Jane believes this is important, she needs reassurance. She also wishes he would not work late so often, as she needs him to be home in the evenings to help her look after their toddler.

However, she does not ask him directly if he loves her. She believes that if she asked him, then of course he would have to say yes, but this would be emotional blackmail and the response might not be genuine. She wants him to say it without prompting, and believes he should know her well enough to do this. John's beliefs are quite different. He believes that as a loving husband and father, he must earn more money working overtime in order to meet the needs of his growing family. He believes that his frequent gifts of flowers to Jane are the best way to show his love for her.

Again there are the same forces at work in their beliefs. Jane believes in mind-reading and also that if she asks, she will not get what she wants. John ignores Jane's protestations that they have enough money: he thinks she's wrong. And both have made different generalizations about how you let another person know you love them.

Like Peter and Jenny, they need to communicate, because they are striving for different things without realizing it. Jane also has to correct her negative beliefs—she cannot expect John to know what she needs if she doesn't tell him.

CHANGE YOUR BELIEFS

In order to eradicate false, negative beliefs, you will have to replace them with true, positive ones. These beliefs will empower you, helping you to achieve more and be happier. The following examples give some indication of how you could change your beliefs. "I'll never be any good at driving," could be replaced with "When I have had enough practice, I will be a good driver." "My friend can't really like me because she hasn't called," can change to "My friend must be busy: I'll call her myself." "Things are terrible and they'll never get any better," could be replaced with "My situation has been difficult in the past, and improved. It will get better now, too."

Untying the knot
False beliefs can form a knot that is very hard to unravel, as one set of distorted beliefs leads to another.

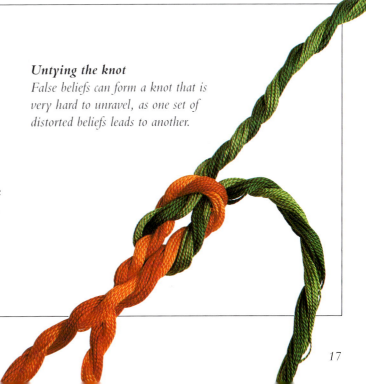

HOW RATIONAL ARE YOU?

How far are your beliefs rational? Do you base them on distortions or generalizations, or are they objectively true? Rational beliefs—based on reason or understanding—are grounded in reality. Read each statement below, and note your immediate response. Then read the commentary under each statement for an analysis of the degree to which the statement is or is not rational.

The general mood

I always know when people are upset: This generalization is full of pitfalls. Perhaps you are often sensitive to other people's moods, but how can you tell this is always the case? Suppose you do not realize that someone is upset because they do not tell you, and you have not gathered it from his or her behavior. Then you would never know, your (mistaken) belief would remain intact, and you might give an inappropriate, if albeit inadvertent, response, doing more harm than good.

How are you feeling?
Assuming you know how other people feel, or expecting them to know what you think without telling them, are beliefs and expectations that will hold you back from real communication.

Can you mind read?

I should not have to tell people when I am upset, they should know: Any belief that involves another person having to guess how you feel, rather than being told, opens the way for misunderstandings. How are they to know? If you appear withdrawn, for example, it is too easy for them to think you are pensive, or simply feel like a quiet time. This belief has the potential for creating highly charged emotional situations when mind reading becomes the evidence for caring.

Open communication is much more effective in meeting your needs: it is easier to tell people around you what you are feeling, whatever that happens to be at the time. Then, they will be able to respond in full possession of the facts—and will be able to offer the support that you require.

Choosing the irrational

It makes me so angry when other people keep me waiting: When anyone says things like "It makes me bored (or miserable, or angry)" they are implying that their feelings are a necessary reaction to a certain event. They are denying any possibility of choice or change in their reactions. This is not rational. Laws of physics such as gravity have an automatic cause and effect, but human beings can change the way they experience things. In fact, you are the person who makes yourself respond in a certain way; nobody and nothing else does.

Do you want to change the way you respond in certain circumstances? Instead of taking it for granted that a situation causes you to feel a certain way, question yourself as to how this happens and ask what would have to happen in order for it not to do so. Then you can look at what steps you can take to make yourself respond differently and take responsibility for your feelings.

A limiting belief

I am not musical: Other clear examples of limiting beliefs include: "I'm no good at mathematics," "I could never stand up and speak in public," and "I'm a terrible dancer." However, music is something you do, not something you are, so your ability to do it can easily change.

You may be generalizing from a few experiences, perhaps from school where you did not succeed in music, according to a teacher or some other expert. However, they may not have been very good at passing on their knowledge. Music is not an all or nothing talent which you either have or do not have. This belief then, could be rephrased more rationally as "When I was at school, I did not succeed in music," or "I find it difficult to sing in tune." And this need not stop you enjoying listening to music.

Distorting the truth

There are such things as winning streaks: This is a distortion of the truth that conveniently ignores the facts. "Winning streaks" are random sequences. For instance, when you toss a coin, the odds for throwing heads or tails is 50-50. Whether four heads or tails in a row are thrown, this has no impact on whether the next coin will come up heads or tails. The odds become higher the more components are added: At present, winning the top prize in the British lottery, where the numbers of six balls have to be guessed, has odds of around 1:17 million.

So although people sometimes do win several times in a row, this has no statistical significance. Gamblers believe in winning streaks some of the time. When they are winning they believe in them; when they are losing, they prefer to believe in the laws of chance, which convince them that they must win soon. A more objective approach would be to calculate statistically the odds of any particular event happening.

An exaggerated view

People are motivated only by money: This is only a partial truth. Here, a reasonable observation—"Some people are motivated only by money"—has been turned into an exaggerated, all-embracing world view.

Which people do you consider are motivated by money, and how sure are you that this is the case? To identify materialism as people's sole motivation, you also need to ignore all the work you have seen yourself and others do for no financial reward.

KNOW WHAT YOU WANT

Remind yourself of things that once seemed impossible when you first considered them, yet which are now achievements on which you look back with satisfaction. Be honest and acknowledge what you really want. Take a few risks and dare to stretch yourself a little. Even if your goals seem a long way off now, setting them and working out a path of progression will bring them closer. Giving yourself something positive to move toward will also motivate you more than focusing on your problems and trying to move away from them.

WHAT DO YOU REALLY WANT from life? This is one of the most fundamental questions we all have to face. Finding the answers is the first step on the way to creating a fulfilling, happy, and rewarding life. You cannot work toward your goals if you do not know what they are, so identifying your aims, hopes, and dreams is vital if you are to achieve what you want.

Set yourself goals

Goal-setting is the key to taking control of your life. You are making choices and creating results in your life all the time, even when you do nothing; the question is, are they the results you want? If you do not set yourself goals, then either chance or other people are likely to determine what you get from life. There are some people who will be delighted to decide for you. They will take charge of your life. Without clear direction and aims of your own, it is all too easy to drift or be influenced by others.

Some people do not set goals because they feel it would inhibit their creativity and spontaneity, but in fact goals provide you with a framework within which you can take risks and try new challenges. Others do not admit what they want because they are afraid of taking a risk, and of feeling foolish and disappointed if they fail. Yet if you have no goals, you will not get what you want anyway.

If you have not already identified your goals, now is the time to start setting them. Try not to limit yourself by what you believe to be currently possible.

The right goals for you

Consider the following questions when setting your goals, to ensure that they are clearly focused and strongly motivating.

• Is your goal expressed in the positive, moving toward what you want, rather than away from something you don't want? Having a negative goal is like going shopping with a list of what you are not going to buy. Any goal that has the words "lose" or "give up" or "don't want" is expressed in the negative. To turn it into a positive one, ask, "What would this goal do for me if I got it?," or "What do I want instead?" For example, "giving up smoking" could become "being more healthy," "being fitter," or "having more money."

• Can you start and maintain your progress toward this goal? What specific things will you have to do? If others need to be involved, ask "How can I ensure that they will help me?"

• Is the goal well defined? Can you see it clearly? Make it as specific as possible. Where and when do you want this goal? In what places and situations and with which people? Set a time scale. The more you can make your outcome specific, the more real it becomes, and the more you will notice and take advantage of opportunities to achieve it.

• How will you know that you have achieved your goal? Be clear about the evidence. How will you feel? What will be different about your life? The evidence defines when you have reached your goal. A race can never end if there is no finishing line.

• What resources do you have to help you achieve this goal? List the possessions, money, people, role models, skills, and personal qualities that will help you achieve your goal.

• What would be the wider consequences and by-products of achieving your goal? Try seeing it from other people's points of view. How does it affect them? What implications might it have? What will you have to sacrifice? Think about the time, money, and effort, both mental and physical, that you will need to invest. Is it worth it? How can you keep what is good about your current circumstances yet still achieve the goal?

• How does your goal relate to your larger plans? What does it help you to achieve and why is this important? It is hard to commit to an outcome that seems unimportant and disconnected from the rest of your life. When you connect your outcome to your values and life plans, it will be motivating.

• Are there smaller goals you need to set to achieve your larger goal? How will you break it down? Are there any obstacles you will have to deal with?

• Does each goal really tie in with what *you* want? Form an action plan, outlining the specific steps you need to take, and including one thing you can do in the next few days. Unless you act, the goal will remain a distant dream.

Toward the future

There will be times when your plans don't come off successfully, or when a change of heart or outside circumstances cause you to rethink your goals. This is only natural and appropriate. Your goals should serve and motivate you, not make you their slave. Keep an open mind and be flexible; you may discover new and unexpected opportunities, talents, and goals if you are open to change.

Taking control of your life means assessing where you are, being clear about where you want to be, and finally using your resources to make sure you get there. Power, influence, and personal fulfillment start with being clear about what you want.

Go for your goals
Set yourself clear, attainable goals, with a structured course of action, and you will achieve them. Defining your goals acts as a motivating force, helping you get off to a good start, achieve your sub-goals along the way, overcome difficulties, and ultimately reach where you want to be.

MEASURE YOUR PLEASURE LEVEL

Perhaps, after you've had an enjoyable evening, you find yourself thinking, "That was great. I really should do this more often." It might seem obvious that if you do more of what you enjoy then you will get more pleasure, yet people often don't take the time to work out what they like best and how they could do more of it. Consciously thinking about the things that give you pleasure—so you can then devote more time to them—is the key to getting more enjoyment out of life. Ask yourself how much pleasure you have now. How many things do you do that you really enjoy? Try the following exercises to assess the pleasure level you derive from the activities and experiences in your life.

Enjoyable experiences

Think of the enjoyable experiences you have had in the past. Start by making a list of up to five pleasant activities under each of the following headings:

1. Environment
2. Travel
3. Sport
4. Hobbies
5. Music
6. Clothes
7. Reading
8. Writing
9. Cooking
10. Television
11. Relaxing
12. Social outings
13. Being with friends
14. Personal relationships
15. Family relationships
16. Meeting new people
17. Children
18. Home and redecorating
19. Giving and receiving gifts
20. Getting on well in your job
21. Telephone conversations
22. Managing your finances/household tasks
23. Problem-solving, your own or others
24. Religious/spiritual activity
25. Sexual activity and feelings

For example, the first category on the list is the environment. Five activities you have done with pleasure under this heading might be: gardening, seeing a beautiful sunset, walking in a forest, being on the beach, and basking in the sun. Examples for another category, say clothes, could be: buying a new pair of shoes, choosing which clothes to put on in the morning, putting on a cosy sweater, window shopping, and feeling attractive in a new outfit.

Identify pleasure patterns

Another way you can identify your favorite activities is to go through the past month in your mind day by day: Try to remember all of the enjoyable things you did, and fit them under the appropriate heading. If you find it difficult to think of any instances at all, it may be because you are looking for experiences that were momentous rather than simply pleasurable. Think small. Remember how the spray of warm water felt on your skin as you took a leisurely shower, or that languid moment in bed just before falling asleep. The days are full of small moments of pleasure like

PLEASURE PRINCIPLES

Enjoyable activities may be broadly divided into three main categories. First, there are those activities that are intrinsically pleasant, such as laughing, eating, sleeping, relaxing, and thinking. Decide on your own three favorites. Many of these activities need no special arrangements; just enjoy them for what they are.

Second, there are those activities that make you feel powerful or competent, such as playing sport, concentrating on a project, planning or learning something new, driving a car. What are your three favorite activities here?

Third, there are activities that involve relating to other people: spending time with friends, sharing with your partner, being understood, praised, appreciated, and thanked. What are your three favorite activities here?

Finally, consider which three of your nine activities give you most self-esteem. How might you include more of these activities in your life?

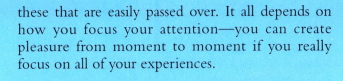

Pleasure overview
Once you have recognized what activities you enjoy most, you must make as much space for them in your life as you can.

these that are easily passed over. It all depends on how you focus your attention—you can create pleasure from moment to moment if you really focus on all of your experiences.

Your pleasure rating

At the end of this exercise you will have a list of up to 125 activities. Now think back over the past month, and rate each item as follows:

Score one if you have not done this activity in the last month.

Score two if you have done this a few times in the last month.

Score three if you have done this several times in the last month.

This gives you a possible maximum of 375 points. How could you increase your score next month? Decide on specific steps you will take to increase your personal pleasure level.

Now rate each item differently:

Score one if you took a little pleasure in it.

Score two if it was moderately pleasant.

Score three if it was very pleasant.

Again, you have a possible maximum total of 375 points. What can you do in order to get a higher score next month? Are there any experiences you would enjoy more if you gave more energy or attention to them? Try this, then assess your rating next month.

THE STRESS FACTOR

Stress has been called the modern disease. The fast pace of modern life, living in cities, high-pressure jobs, increasing job insecurity, and the accelerating pace of change in all areas of our lives can all contribute to mounting feelings of stress, which in turn can lead to stress-related illnesses.

The term stress derives from engineering. A structure subjected to strain can withstand it by yielding until it reaches a "breakpoint," at which point it collapses. This analogy when applied to humans suggests that people cope with pressure up to a certain point and then break down—either psychologically or physically. But pressure in itself is not a bad thing. A healthy amount of stress can stimulate, motivate, and keep us alert and interested in life. In fact, a complete lack of challenges is stressful in itself. Problems arise when the challenges are greater than an individual feels able to cope with, which can manifest itself in feelings of distress and, for some, a wide range of worrying symptoms.

Fight or flight

Stress triggers a physical reaction known as the "fight or flight" response, which all creatures experience when confronted with a threat. The symptoms are always the same: the heartbeat and breathing rate increase, blood pressure goes up, blood rushes away from the digestive system to the muscles of the arms and legs to prepare the body for immediate action, and the pupils of the eyes dilate. In everyday life we face dozens of small threats such as criticism, deadlines, and traffic—our bodies experience them all as potential dangers and react accordingly. When the fight or flight response is triggered, your body produces stress hormones, including adrenaline, that send you into overdrive. If you are unable to find release in action, or if the fight or flight response occurs repeatedly without time to wind down in between, your body remains in a state of heightened awareness.

Stop carrying the load
Too much stress can weigh you down. Recognize the symptoms and you can start to deal with it.

Too much stress can erode people's ability to cope with their everyday tasks. For example, Kevin has a challenging job. He has to deal with queries from the public, soothe disgruntled customers, please a demanding boss, and work to tight deadlines. Most of the time he enjoys rising to the challenge and says he gets satisfaction from "keeping all the balls in the air." Some weeks ago, however, his mother became seriously ill and every weekend Kevin travels 200 miles to see her. This added stress has taken its toll, and recently, Kevin has found it difficult to keep his temper with "whining customers," and finds it hard to concentrate on his latest report although the deadline is nearly up. Kevin's ability to manage has been undermined by the number of stressful events that he has to face at once.

The causes of stress fall into two main categories. Psychologists Thomas Holmes and Richard Rahe found that major life events such as moving house, marriage, birth and, particularly, death all cause stress. Furthermore, this type of stress is cumulative—the more of these events that occur within a two-year period, the more likely you are to be adversely affected. Another researcher, Dr. Richard Lazarus, found that minor traumatic events or hassles can be equally stressful if you have to deal with too many of them at once.

Controlling stress

How you deal with stressors depends on how much control you have over them. The more control, the less stress. This contradicts the popular image of the stressed-out executive. Research suggests that the higher the status of the job, the less the stress. For example, factory floor workers, because they have less control over their jobs than chief executives, face greater stress. What is seen as stimulating to one person may be highly stressful to another. Personality and emotional makeup also influence the way in which we react to stress-inducing events. Research has revealed that some people are far hardier than others when it comes to dealing with stress. As in a building, stability and flexibility are essential attributes when responding to pressure.

STRESS SYMPTOMS

What are the symptoms that are associated with high levels of stress? In organizations the effects of stress among employees can be seen in increasing absenteeism, a decline in the quality of the work done and morale, and an increase in accidents and complaints.

Listed below are some of the physical symptoms that medical practitioners believe have a link with stress.

Mild: wet hands/perspiration, indigestion/dyspepsia, palpitations, rashes, dryness in mouth, acid/bile rising, pains in chest, eye flickering, cold sores, mouth ulcers, backache/neckache, headaches

Severe: heart conditions, hypertension, stomach ulcers, irritable bowel syndrome, asthma, eczema, arthritis, liver disease, severe headaches/migraine, ME

STRESS CHECKLIST

Knowing the symptoms of stress, both physical and psychological, is the first step in stress management. These "early warning signals" are a cue to take action and deal with the root cause of the stress (see pp. 26-27).

1. Do you often feel panicky for no specific reason? Do you experience feelings of impending disaster without apparent cause?

2. Have your sleeping patterns changed? Are you sleeping a lot more or a lot less? Do you wake up in the night unable to go back to sleep? Do you feel tired all the time?

3. Are you arguing a lot more or a lot less than usual with your partner?

4. Have you lost interest in sex?

5. Have you gone off your food or are you eating more than usual?

6. Do you find it difficult to concentrate at work and/or difficult to complete things that you start?

7. Are you avoiding people for no particular reason?

8. Are you smoking or drinking considerably more than usual?

9. Are you subject to sharp swings in your moods or are you more irritable or depressed than usual?

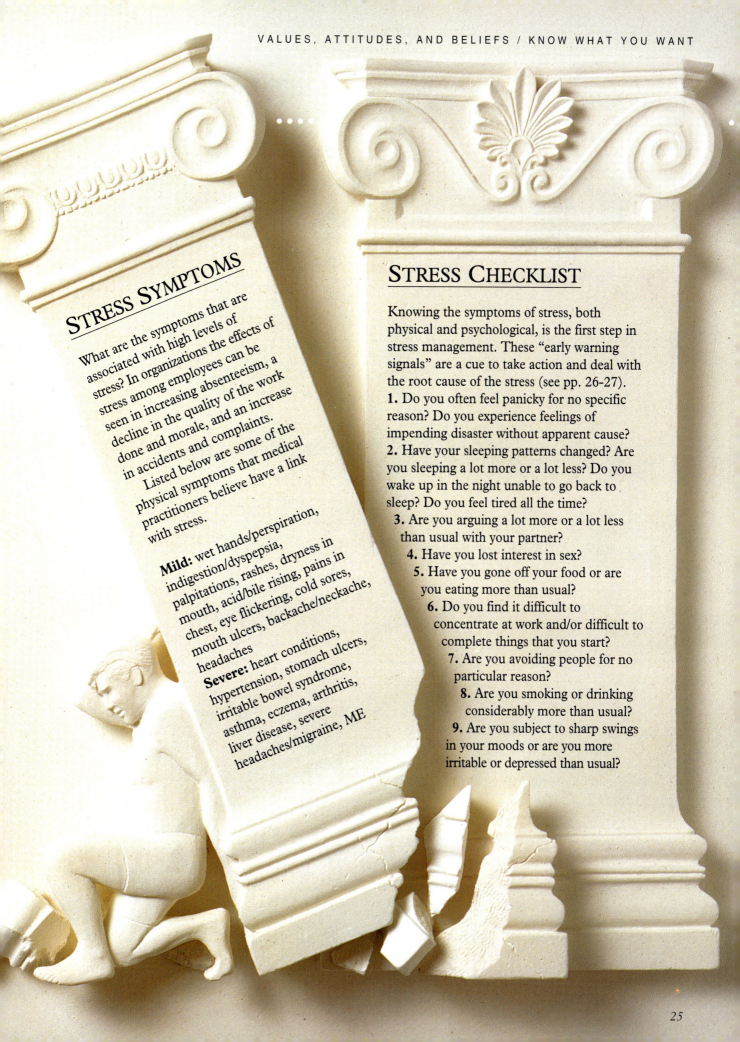

COPING WITH STRESS

Some people remain relatively unaffected by the harmful effects of stress. Research indicates that they share certain personal characteristics and skills, including problem-solving abilities that they bring to bear on their own lives. In one study, researchers from the University of Chicago found that people who coped best with stress had three things in common: They were committed to and excited by their work, they felt in control of their lives, and they embraced and were stimulated by change. People who cope well with stress realize that no one can expect everything—or everyone—to be perfect all the time. They accept imperfection as a fact of life and do not brood over "injustice," or drive themselves in search of perfection.

Be assertive

If other people are the cause of your stress, learn how to handle them assertively. Be prepared to confront difficult and unpleasant issues by expressing your feelings openly and skilfully. Learn to cope with the fact that you cannot be popular with everyone in every situation. Some people who are

The stresses of life
When the pace of modern life seems overwhelming, stop and take time to assess the situation realistically.

highly stressed squander much of their energy on being troubled by others' perception of them. Remember, no one can please everyone all of the time, so settle for pleasing "some of the people some of the time."

Take Jenny, for example, who feels that, because she did not finish university, she must outdo all the others in her office to prove she's not a failure. She therefore works very long hours and takes on extra responsibility. During a discussion with one of her colleagues, he points out to her that she is the only one who feels that she has to prove something; everyone else accepts her work on its merits. In fact, she discovers that several people she thought had degrees have a less formal education than she does. Armed with this different perspective, Jenny takes a less "driven" approach to her work.

Learning to prioritize

Stress at home will impact on work and vice versa. If you are working very long hours to meet a deadline, you may find yourself giving your family's needs a lower priority than your work. On the other hand, if you have a family crisis, you may need temporarily to devote more time to your family and less to your job. Knowing what your priorities are at any given time can help you avoid stress. Those who cope best with a busy, stressful life are prepared to devote a substantial effort to achievement, but they maintain a balanced lifestyle.

One of the most important skills in avoiding stress is time management. The build-up and pace of stressful events can be controlled by realistic planning and intervention. Do not commit yourself to excessively tight schedules that are unlikely to be met. Say no! This is a professional attitude and other people will respect it. Where possible, delegate. The alternative may result in a struggle to meet almost impossible commitments, with the accompanying stress.

Rest and relaxation

Studies have shown that exercise reduces anxiety and muscular tension. People who exercise aerobically for at least 30 minutes four or five times a week find that their pulse rates return to normal more quickly after participating in stressful events. Relaxation triggers the opposite of the stress response—breathing rates slow down and blood pressure is lowered, getting rid of the negative effects of stress. Choose the type of exercise or relaxation that is most appropriate for you and your lifestyle. Some people find going for a run after a hectic and stressful day at work is an excellent way to "run off" any of their pent-up frustrations. Others wind down by doing some yoga every day, which they find extremely relaxing and calming.

STRESS AWARENESS

One of the causes of stress is change—good or bad. This quiz will help you to identify the amount of stress that you have experienced. If a particular event listed below has happened to you within the last two years, score the event according to the value given to it. The higher you score, the more likely you are to be suffering from stress. For more detailed analysis of your score, see pages 138-139.

Life event	Value
Death of a partner	100
Divorce	73
Separation	65
Death of a family member *(not a partner)*	63
Major injury or illness	53
Marriage	50
Losing job	47
Retirement	45
Reconciliation with partner	45
Pregnancy *(own or partner's)*	40
A new baby in the family	39
Elderly relatives moving in	39
Death of a close friend	37
Starting a new job	36
Taking on a mortgage	31
Major changes at work	29
Son/daughter leaves home	29
Partner starts/stops work	26
Moving house	25

Total score

A chain of events

As we progress through life, we all collect experiences, some of them positive, some of them negative. Any change can be stressful, even a welcomed one.

MASTER YOURSELF

"NO MAN IS FREE who is not master of himself," wrote the Greek philosopher Epictetus. But in order to "master yourself," you must know who you are. Each of us has been formed by the varied experiences—many of them absorbed deep into the unconscious—that have bombarded us since birth. Understanding precisely how you have been shaped by your different experiences is a major step toward mastering how you respond to events in your life.

Ghosts from the past

How often have you been in a situation where you have felt strangely uncomfortable and yet there seems to be no logical explanation for this negative feeling? Your unease could well be due to an earlier, forgotten occasion when you found yourself in a similar situation and had every reason to feel discomfort. This "lost" experience is still triggering a certain response in you long after the original event has passed, and your reaction is now beyond

your conscious awareness. In these situations you are not deliberately choosing to act in a certain way, you are functioning on "automatic pilot." These automatic reactions may enhance your life, or they may act against you. When things seem to be going wrong and you can't immediately find out why, it's time to look at the experiences that have led to your present circumstances.

Think of your automatic responses. While it is entirely appropriate to carry out many activities, such as touch-typing or driving a car, on automatic pilot, you may feel there are times when your response does not suit the stimuli. For example, if you worry yourself sick whenever you have to speak in front of others, take the time to think back and analyze past occasions on which you have spoken in public. Try and discover the root cause of your fears. Can you identify a time when your

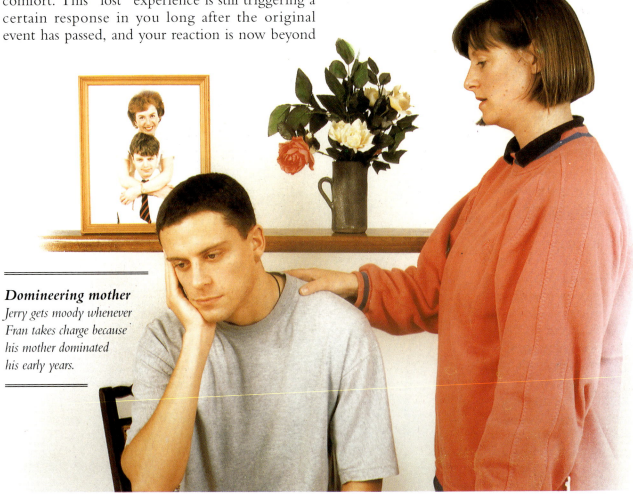

Domineering mother
Jerry gets moody whenever Fran takes charge because his mother dominated his early years.

anxieties were justified—perhaps you were afraid of being put down in public by a critical partner or boss? If you are now happy in your job, and know that your fears of criticism are unfounded, then your anxiety is linked to this bad experience.

Get back in control

Suzie couldn't understand why she felt hostile toward her boyfriend, Tom, when he occasionally called her Suzanne instead of the usual Suzie. She asked herself some searching questions, such as, "What does this feeling remind me of?" She realized that she was re-experiencing the fear she had felt as a child when her authoritarian father had disciplined her for some misdemeanor. He had always called her Suzanne on these occasions, not the more affectionate Suzie. This realization helped her to control her emotional response to Tom. The example of Suzie shows that, if you use your consciousness to examine the building blocks of your experiences, then you can achieve a far greater mastery of your responses—and of your whole life.

IMPRINTED BEHAVIOR

The behavioral scientist Konrad Lorenz used the word "imprint" to refer to the process by which young animals and humans attach themselves to someone—or something—at a critical stage in their development. He made studies of ducklings and discovered that as soon as they hatched they looked for a mother figure. If the ducklings were shown something other than their real mother at this early stage, they would follow it. If the mother was brought back later, they would ignore her and follow the object they had "imprinted."

There is evidence that imprinting may affect humans during the early part of their lives. Jerry, for example, grew up with a domineering mother. He vowed that he would never marry anyone like her, but when he married Fran she quickly took over his life. Luckily, Jerry became aware that he had married a version of his mother. He also realized that Fran was *not* his mother and learned to separate the relationships. He then managed to change the balance of his relationship with Fran.

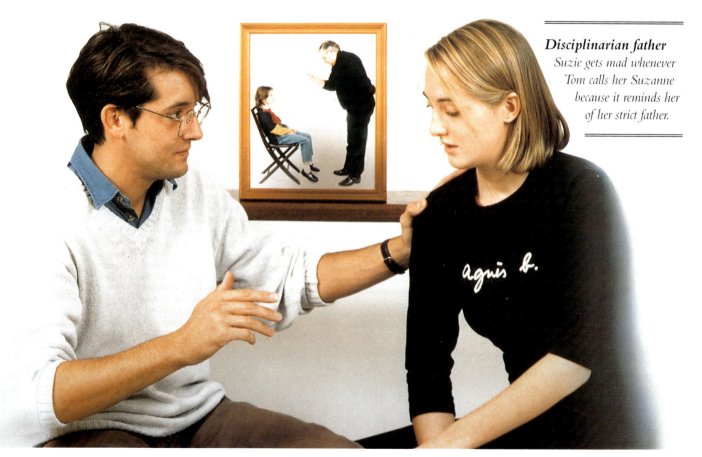

Disciplinarian father
Suzie gets mad whenever
Tom calls her Suzanne
because it reminds her
of her strict father.

WHAT IS AN "EXPERIENCE"?

Understanding our experiences can bring greater self-knowledge, but what is an "experience?" Most people probably never stop to think what experiences actually are—they believe that they simply "have them." However, once you understand the nature of your experiences and start to unravel their component parts, you will be even more able to take control of your life.

Where does it all begin?

An experience begins by activating one or more of your five senses—sight, hearing, smell, taste, and touch. Your brain interprets this reaction as pleasurable or unpleasurable sensations, thoughts, feelings, and desires.

These sensations and feelings are enormously important. They act as an internal monitor, telling us how well or badly we think things are going for us, and so we should listen to them very attentively. Too often people concentrate on the nuts and bolts of an experience, what "happened," and ignore the vital end-product—how they feel about the event.

Feelings are a highly personal matter, and if two people undergo exactly the same experience, they will probably have very different feelings at the end of it. There are several reasons for this: each person has their own personal portfolio of previous experiences and memories; and each person has an unconscious preference for one or two of the senses over the others. For example, many people depend greatly on the spoken word when they take in their experiences of the world. To them, the sounds of an experience will be of particular significance.

The world of the senses

This sensory approach has been developed much further by practitioners of NLP (Neuro-Linguistic Programming), who also maintain that each of us has a "primary" sense. This is the sense we automatically prefer when we think consciously about an event. So, if when your are recalling a particularly

enjoyable summer vacation, you remember the crashing of the waves and the cries of the gulls' most clearly, your primary sense is auditory.

Each of us also has a "lead" sense. This is the sense we prefer to bring information to our mind—the initial trigger for our thoughts. So, if when you recall a recent vacation, the very first thing that comes to you, before the sounds of the place take over, are the smells—of the food, of the flowers—your lead sense is kinesthetic (see "Clues and Cues" opposite).

Your lead sense might vary depending on the type of experience. For example, the sense of touch might trigger unpleasant experiences, and some kind of visual picture might lead you into happy ones.

Making sense of experience

Think about having a cup of coffee. Is it the sight of the swirl of cream, the taste, the smell, the feel of the hot cup, or the sound of a stirring spoon that comes to mind?

CLUES AND CUES

Over the next couple of days jot down the kinds of words you, and others, use and try these NLP exercises. Examining your language will help you to identify your primary sense:

- **The visual person** (thinks in pictures). They use phrases such as "I see," or "Focus on this."
- **The auditory person** (thinks in sounds). They may say "That rings a bell," or "That echoes something that happened last year."
- **The kinesthetic person** (thinks in terms of how they feel, a more physical approach that involves touch, taste, and smell). They might say "I feel optimistic today," or "I can handle it."

Another way that you might be able to tell which sense is uppermost is to use what NLP calls "visual accessing cues." NLP practitioners have found that people's eyes tend to move in a certain direction if their thoughts are led by a specific sense, which are as follows:

- **Looking up** means that the person is "picturing" something—they are using their visual sense.
- **Looking to either side** indicates that the auditory sense is in use.
- **Looking down** may suggest kinesthetic senses. Watch others and see if their eyes often move in one direction—and get them to watch you!

Personal preferences

Find out your preferred sense or senses by discussing a shared event with others. Think about your last vacation and try to decide what your lead and primary senses are. If you went on vacation with other people—family, friends, a partner—ask them for their sensory impressions. Did they pay particular attention to the same things as you? Soon you will discover just how much people's sensory makeup differs.

Making your senses work for you

By appreciating that experiences come to us via our favored senses, we can become much more effective in our lives. For example, if you have never realized how much you think in terms of seeing, and you are trying to learn something by using audio-based materials, you may find that turning to visual teaching aids will make all the difference.

You can also improve your relationships with others. If you are explaining something to someone with a strong auditory connection, but you respond primarily to touch, communication may be easier if you adjust your language to suit each other's preferred system (see "Clues and Cues" above). Once you are more aware of your senses, you might even develop underused ones in order to make your experiences much richer.

Before long, you may find the words of Anthony Robbins, in *Unlimited Power*, coming true: "Before we can direct our experiences of life, we must first understand how we experience."

THE POWER OF THE MIND

HOW POSSIBLE IS IT to control your own brain—to think and feel the way you would like to, rather than feeling prey to unwanted thoughts? One approach that many people have found useful in changing their negative self-beliefs and reinforcing positive ones is NLP (Neuro-Linguistic Programming).

The way we internally represent experiences to ourselves is examined from an NLP point of view on pages 30–31. But there is more to understanding your experiences than knowing that you prefer to think in terms of visual cues, sounds, or feelings. You also need to be aware of the details of your experience. One way to do this is to look at what are known in NLP as your "submodalities," which are described in the box, below.

As you describe an experience to yourself, listen to the words that you are using. Do you hear yourself making apologies and offering excuses or blaming everybody else? Look out for expressions such as, "He made me behave like that," or "Why does this always happen to me?" Look, too, at the feelings that are attached to the recollection. Perhaps you had to repress your feelings, or maybe

EXAMINE THE DETAIL

It is important to understand how you construct positive and negative experiences in your mind so that you can manipulate them to your advantage. To do this, try to bring into your mind a positive memory and make a note of what you see, hear, or feel. Look at the construction of your mental image of the situation—its color, dimension, timescale, and focus. What form does the image take? Is it in black and white or in color? Is it close up or far away? Is it two dimensional or three dimensional? Is the image fleeting or persistent? Is it clear and focused, or blurred and indistinct? Is there any sound involved? Do you experience any sensations? Can you feel a different energy level in your body? Now do the same with a negative memory.

Most people find that when they examine their submodalities of important memories, good and bad, they are very strong and vivid, whereas those of less significant events are dimmer. Visually led people, for example, report that they see an important memory as a moving film, in color, and very close up. More significantly, they see themselves in the experience. If you want to enhance a happy memory, try to alter it so that it is more colorful, closer to you, and includes you in the picture. Then take an unhappy experience and take yourself outside it so that you are a viewer. Push the experience away from you until it is small, in black and white, and static, like a photograph. You may now find that you feel less emotional about it.

Playing with pictures
There are many different ways of seeing the same object. By controlling how you see things you can determine whether an experience is negative or positive.

you lost your temper? What was your reaction to the mistakes that you feel you made? Was it really appropriate to the actual error?

Examining your physiology can also reveal a lot about your internal world. Try to bring into your mind an experience when you failed to achieve something that you set out to do. Talk about the event to yourself. Is your inner voice quiet and dull, does it sound monotonous and complaining? Direct your attention to your hands, neck, and face. Are they relaxed or tense? Try to feel the muscles in your face and become aware of your expression.

Then think of a positive experience, and take yourself through the same self-examination. You may find that your voice sounds steady and firm. Do the words you use suggest that you have taken responsibility for your actions? If you have, your language will be positive and to the point. It will allow for other people's opinions, and work constructively toward a solution.

Remember, it is the way that you think about events that gives them an emotional dimension. The next time you find a negative situation, use what you have learnt to enhance your positive feelings.

ARE YOU HOLDING BACK?

If you feel you are failing to live up to your potential in one or more areas of your life, an important factor may be that you are holding yourself back in some way from confronting situations you may see as problematic. This way of dealing with (or, more accurately, failing to deal with) difficult or sensitive situations is one that almost everyone employs at some time, and is explored by American psychologist Susan Jeffers in her book *Feel the Fear and Do It Anyway*. The following questionnaire will help you to identify those aspects of your own life that may be suffering from your inability to take the necessary action. For each question, score one for a response of Usually, two for Often, three for Sometimes, and four if your answer is Never.

Trembling on the brink
Are you holding yourself back from experiencing life to the full? Self-limiting behavior can take on many guises, but the resulting feeling of powerlessness is common to all.

1. Do you blame your partner, family, friends, boss, personal jinx, or anything apart from yourself for the things that make you unhappy ?

2. Do you expect a certain level of love, commitment, interest, or loyalty from those close to you, and lose motivation if you don't get it?

3. Do you find that you are often resentful, judgmental or critical toward others?

4. Do you attempt to control the people around you at home and at work?

5. To put off taking decisive action, do you resort to excuses such as, "I can't make a start on X until I've finished Y"?

6. Do you shy away from confronting awkward or difficult situations?

7. Do you worry unduly about making mistakes?

8. Do you stick stubbornly to one path once you have made your choice?

9. Do you tend to take what you feel is the "right" course of action, rather than doing what you really want to do?

10. Are you motivated by guilt?

11. Do you worry about what might happen in all kinds of hypothetical scenarios?

12. Do you avoid making changes or taking risks?

HOW DID YOU SCORE?

24-48 If your score falls in this range, you are not just holding yourself back—you have virtually brought yourself to a standstill. Feeling powerless to make any difference to either your own life or the world around you, you have lost much of your zest for living. Take the first steps toward changing your life by reading "Stop Holding Back" on pages 36-37.

49-72 If your score falls in the middle range, you have probably achieved some degree of self-determination, so why not take it all the way? You realize there is much more you can make of your life, but you lack enough genuine self-confidence to push yourself that bit further. Remember, at first it will be hard work to overcome your fears and try to make the most of every opportunity. But once you have experienced the satisfaction of taking control, you will find that it becomes second nature.

73-96 If your score is in this group, you are already well aware that you can't just sit around and wait for life to come to you—you have to go out and seize it with both hands. Whatever happens, you are confident that you will be able to deal with it, and maybe gain something from the experience. You have already learned the most important lesson of all—that a strong belief in yourself has the potential to move mountains.

13. Do you run yourself down and assume blame for things that are in no way your fault?

14. Do you expect a great deal from others, and keep track of every favor you give or are given?

15. Are you bored, dissatisfied, frustrated, or disappointed with your life?

16. Do you fail to support deserving causes because you feel powerless to make any difference to society or the environment?

17. Do you dwell on your vulnerability?

18. Do you behave as though life were a constant struggle?

19. Do you dislike spending time alone, preferring to be with people, whether you like them or not?

20. Do you concentrate on one part of your life at the expense of others?

21. Do you find it hard to set goals because you lack a sense of purpose?

22. Do you listen to an inner voice that tells you that you are incompetent or destined for failure?

23. Do you find it difficult to let yourself go in order to relax and enjoy yourself?

24. Do you avoid looking at anything beyond your own day-to-day existence?

STOP HOLDING BACK

Fear holds everyone back in one or more areas of their lives. It might be fear of showing emotion, fear of failure, fear of being alone, or any of countless other examples. Whatever the cause of the fear, however, it always has the same result. It paralyzes people, and stops them from achieving what they want by preventing them from taking even the first steps toward their goal.

In *Feel the Fear and Do It Anyway*, Susan Jeffers develops an approach that shows people how to break through this barrier. Rather than denying that you feel fear, and waiting for it to go away, she suggests that you should acknowledge the fear—and do it anyway. This isn't about recklessly indulging in dangerous pursuits; it is about pushing through the smaller fears that invade your everyday life, lowering your self-esteem and preventing you from moving forward. Remember, everyone is afraid of something, but not everyone allows this to restrict them. Fear isn't the problem—it's how we deal with it that counts, and you can deal with it constructively in all kinds of ways.

Spring into action

Only if you do something about your situation will you break the cycle of fear and apathy. Just thinking about it achieves nothing. Even if your action seems a small one, it could represent a huge psychological leap. Soon, decisive action will become a habit, not a hurdle. Jeffers suggests getting a taste of wider horizons by taking one very small risk every day. Try telling someone how you feel, talk to a neighbor you usually ignore, or say no to a favor you do not want to do.

Taking action shows that you are taking responsibility for your life, and not sitting around blaming others or seeing how you can get them to do what you should be doing yourself. Shoulder the responsibility for the rough as well as the smooth, then you will be where you should be—in control.

Making it happen

How you set about taking action is all-important. First, decide on your goal(s) and gather information. However large or small your action is, give it everything you've got. Anything entered into half-heartedly has less chance of working out, and gives you the perfect excuse not to try again.

Don't waste time and energy trying to imagine exactly how things will be if you take a certain course of action—and worrying about whether you could deal with it. If you do, you risk shutting yourself off from opportunities before they happen. Just say to yourself that, regardless of the situation, you will be able to cope. Concentrate on making the best of whatever happens. This doesn't mean staying on a certain path simply because you have invested a lot of energy in it. Give it a good shot and, if things aren't working, try something else. Then, however things turn out, you are in charge.

This kind of positive thinking is the key to launching yourself out into the world. In his book *Unlimited Power*, Anthony Robbins talks about "reframing" situations—in other words, choosing to look at things in a more positive light. For example, if you are deciding between staying with a partner and ending the relationship, don't automatically view the first option as a dead-end because it doesn't seem to represent moving on in life. Instead, think about what action you could take to improve things between the two of you.

Positive power operates in other ways too. Language plays a huge role in reinforcing how we feel. If you use positive, assertive language—"I won't" rather than "I can't"; "It's a challenge" and not "It's a problem"—you will slowly reprogram yourself so that you feel optimistic and strong. Also, dealing with those around you in a positive way reaps enormous rewards. If you radiate warmth, trust, interest, and love, and give without expecting thanks, you attract the same qualities in return and will find all kinds of doors opening to you. Your self-esteem will flourish. The nagging, negative little voice inside your head that constantly holds you back will begin to fade away and you will discover that you feel much happier.

Something that holds many people back is placing too much emphasis on one particular area of their life—especially work and partners—at the expense of other areas. Your life should be as rounded as possible, including friends, family, partners, work, leisure, working for a cause you believe in—and yourself. If you give yourself wholeheartedly to each of these, your world will not collapse when, for example, you lose a job or partner, and you will be better equipped to move on.

With a little help...

There are all kinds of tools that will help you to stop holding back. You might decide to join a self-help group, read further on the subject, or listen to some of the tapes that you can buy, especially first thing in the morning or last thing at night. Many of these tapes feature visualization sequences, but you can create your own visualization by lying down in a quiet room, closing your eyes, and imagining what it would feel like to stop holding yourself back. Pinning notices that carry positive messages around your home or office is also highly effective, as is repeating out loud positive phrases such as "I do make a difference."

Take the plunge
Taking a risk, no matter how small, is the antidote to the paralyzing effects of fear—action will help you to stop holding back and start living.

DON'T VICTIMIZE YOURSELF

Y ou will probably have heard, and given some credence to, the saying that someone is "one of life's natural victims." Indeed, everyone feels and behaves like a victim sometimes—perhaps you feel you spend all your time doing things you don't really want to do, or comparing yourself unfavorably to others.

But no one needs to be a victim. You may feel unhappy and unfulfilled and believe that you are being victimized by all manner of things—your partner, family, boss, or upbringing. But it is not circumstances that determine whether or not you allow yourself to be a victim, but how you choose to deal with them.

Assert yourself

There are all kinds of ways in which you can stop yourself from being a victim. Perhaps the most important thing is to be really clear what you want before problems arise. Take an active role in shaping events—don't let things just "happen" to you.

Life is full of situations which can leave you feeling that people have taken advantage of you. But it is up to you to avoid falling into the victim trap. For example, if you complain about a dish at a restaurant and staff respond defensively, remember they are trained to rebuff complaints. Don't take what they say personally, or become aggressive—they are simply paid to carry out company policy. Don't start to sink into victim mode if they try to fob you off with irrelevant comparisons such as, "Well, no one has complained before." Simply say, politely, "I'm not really interested in that; I've got this specific complaint now." Even when you may find it difficult to assert yourself, such as in dealings with your boss, it is possible to stand your ground. For example, if your boss asks you to stay late on a night you have an important date with a friend, don't just say yes and inwardly feel annoyed. Explain why you really can't stay this particular night unless it is very urgent. Offer to come in early the next morning or try to reach a useful compromise.

A prison of your own making?
However impossible a situation may appear to be, examine it carefully—are you, in effect, acting as your own jailer? You may well find on further investigation that you have more choices than at first seem obvious.

The victim scenario

Sometimes people find that, almost without realizing it, they have become locked into the role of victim. This is destructive for both the victim and the victimizer. Take the case of Judy and her eldest daugher, Tessa. Judy suffered from the most terrible headaches that left her unable to do anything for days. These often occurred when she felt under stress, but she had never really got to the root of what was causing them.

Judy's problem put the whole family under great pressure. Her husband had a very busy job, so it was left to Tessa to keep things running when her mother was ill. The situation was not healthy for either Judy or Tessa. Judy wasn't sorting out the cause of her illness or finding a treatment for it. She was using illness to hide her inability to cope and had also grown to enjoy the attention her illness brought her.

Tessa felt guilty because she was allowed to believe that she and the other children were in some way the cause of their mother's headaches. She was missing out on growing up and her education. She also felt responsible for resolving a problem that she would never be able to solve. This in turn lowered her self-esteem, leaving her less able to deal with the situation.

Making the break

Then, suddenly, Tessa was invited on a last-minute free foreign holiday by her grandmother. The day before Tessa was due to leave, Judy came down with a headache, but the tickets had been booked and Tessa went anyway. Getting away helped Tessa to see the situation from a different perspective. For the first time she felt able to discuss her frustrations with another person, her grandmother, who pointed out that Tessa would not be selfish to put her own priorities higher up the list.

Soon afterward, Tessa announced that she was thinking of postponing her education, moving out, and getting a job because she could not cope with her studies. Judy was horrified. She at last realized that she was driving her daughter away, and more than anything she wanted her daughter to complete her education. Judy at last took action to resolve her problem and sought treatment, taking pressure off her daughter.

LEARNING TO SAY NO

Being unable to say no is at the root of much self-victimization. If you want to escape your self-made trap, you must get into the habit of saying this both to yourself and—clearly and assertively —to others. Say no to these things in your life:
• thinking of yourself as a victim or as a weak/incapable/stupid/unattractive person when compared to others or in the face of institutions or the world in general
• letting others make you feel inferior, especially when they use accusatory, guilt-inducing language such as "You should have..."
• expecting to fail before you even begin a task
• always putting yourself and your enjoyment of life last and taking no time for yourself
• allowing others to dictate what you should do
• blaming others or avoiding personal responsibility because you feel others could always do a better job than you could
• worrying about what others think of you
• expecting everyone to like you; being upset if people don't agree with you or if you have to confront people.

Saying no to being a victim means saying yes to being a happy, confident, and positive person. The basis of a self-empowering plan of action is to think of yourself as a potent person, to pinpoint the types of situation in which you turn into a victim, and to develop an outlook that will stand you in good stead whenever you are faced with potentially victimizing situations.

Release yourself
Learn to say no and
free yourself from all
the limitations of
self-victimization.

CHAPTER TWO

FAMILIES, WORK, AND RELATIONSHIPS

HOW YOU DEAL with some of the core difficulties you encounter in life—conflict within the family, a relationship running far from smoothly, a job that is a source of anxiety or unfulfillment—is inevitably affected by your early conditioning. Understanding this, while at the same time acquiring the adult skills to deal with your problems, are the tools you need to resolve any complications in these three fundamental areas.

We start by taking a closer look at the family—always a potential source of problems in our lives, past and present. This is especially true when various family members hold strongly differing points of view—a dilemma explored in "Family Scenarios" on pages 42-43. Identifying your particular family type (pp. 44-45) is essential in gaining some kind of understanding about how you were affected by your family while you were growing up. The impact of these early building blocks in later life is examined in more detail on pages 46-47.

The workplace is another significant area of activity in our lives, not least with regard to job fulfillment. We look at some of the reasons behind discontent at work, and how you might address a change. If you feel it is time for a move,

the quiz on pages 52-53 "Are You in the Right Job?" may help to clarify the situation. Perhaps your problem is not so much lack of interest or focus as interpersonal issues; "Can You Cope with Authority?" (pp. 54-55) addresses this thorny question directly and helpfully.

Our personal relationships are vital to a sense of well-being. In "Managing Relationships" (pp. 58-59) we look first of all at exactly what constitutes a good, interdependent relationship, and offer some guidelines on what to do when a relationship runs into trouble. Many relationship difficulties center around dependency—either being afraid of being too dependent, and therefore keeping your distance, or wanting all your needs to be met from one source: your partner. Either way, the relationship will suffer. Spotting "Signs of Over-dependence" (pp. 62-63) explains some of the reasons behind our dependency needs, such as low self-esteem, and an inability to get in touch with our needs and wants. Where dependency has become entrenched, the co-dependency trap looms—the "carer" and the "victim," often with addiction problems, are enmeshed in a dance of dependency that must be broken if anything is to change.

GAINING INSIGHT INTO WHAT LIES BEHIND ANY DIFFICULTIES AT HOME, IN RELATIONSHIPS, AND IN THE WORKPLACE, ARE THE FIRST ESSENTIAL STEPS TO RESTORING A SENSE OF CONTROL.

FAMILY SCENARIOS

Different points of view
It can be hard for the family to accept that individual members have their own ideas about how to conduct their lives. Conflict and misunderstandings often occur when potential difficulties arise.

result of gradual change and development in a couple or partnership. The following scenarios show how easily conflict can arise when family members see a situation from totally different points of view.

Freedom or license?

Teenagers often challenge family rulings. This is because they are seeking to understand and establish their own personality, and may use the family standards as a "wall to kick against."

Simon had been told several times that he would be grounded if he persisted in coming home late after evenings out with his friends. His parents, Mike and Sally, worried when he came home much later than they allowed him, because Sally was concerned at the thought of him walking home alone in the dark. Mike told Simon *he* had never been allowed such freedom when he was 16. Simon, for his part, felt his parents were being unreasonable because his friends were less restricted and he resented returning home before they had to. The problem will continue as long as Simon and his parents both believe they are in the right and refuse to see the other's point of view. If they can recognize each other's needs, they may then be able to reach a compromise arrangement that they can all accept.

Standing alone or unsupported?

Problems that develop between children and parents don't only stem from the child's blindness to parental responsibilities, but might also arise from parents' inability to understand that their children may be different from themselves. This may make it difficult for them to see their children's needs.

Mark had been bullied at school for several weeks before admitting the problem to his father.

MOST PEOPLE, IF ASKED, would say that they usually try to foster a lifestyle that meets the needs of all the members of the family. However, behavior that can seem helpful to one person can seem unhelpful to another: Many adults have vivid childhood memories of being told that doing something they disliked was for their own good— from eating their vegetables to taking medicine. In children, this problem of a conflicting viewpoint can sometimes be attributed to an inability to understand the wider responsibilities that an adult must carry. In adult relationships within the family unit, however, a difference of view is often the

Mark's father wanted to do his best for Mark, but had privately sometimes felt his son was "too soft." He therefore saw the bullying as a chance to help his son toughen up, and encouraged him to give as good as he got. Mark was a shy and sensitive boy who felt unable to do as his father said. This in turn left him feeling misunderstood and unsupported. Eventually a teacher helped him to sort out the problem. But while Mark felt his father had let him down, Mark's father continued to see the situation differently, believing Mark had learnt a valuable lesson. It was only later, at a school parents' evening, as Mark's father listened to the teacher's assessment of the problem, that he began to understand his son's point of view.

Protected or deceived?

It is often very hard to imagine what another person's point of view might be. It is especially difficult when you are trying to work out how someone might interpret your own actions or behavior, because there is a danger that you will assume they see things the same way you do.

Josie had been living with her partner, Sam, for some time when she had an affair with a mutual friend. The liaison was short-lived, and Josie managed to conceal the whole episode from Sam. Secretly, Josie was deeply ashamed of her infidelity, and rationalized her guilt by telling herself that she should keep the affair secret, as finding out would hurt Sam deeply. Some time later, however, her ex-lover told Sam about their affair. Sam told Josie he could see little future for the two of them and their relationship broke down completely. He explained that he might have recovered from Josie's affair had she admitted her mistake, but that he had found her deception much harder to take. He did not feel that she had acted to protect him, but that she had betrayed him. By lying to him, Sam felt that Josie had fundamentally undermined their relationship. He questioned Josie's integrity in other areas of their life together, and wondered what other secrets she was withholding from him.

Reconciling different points of view

Most family or partnership situations can be seen from both a positive and a negative perspective. It is often a sense of unfairness or injustice that causes a partner or a child to view a certain situation as being loaded against him or her. Helping each person to understand the reasoning behind certain behavior, whilst inviting them to contribute to family decisions, can help to maintain a sense of balance and offset many of the problems that beset families. It is important to remember when taking such an approach that it requires patience and commitment—the temptation to take shortcuts should be firmly resisted.

IDENTIFY YOUR FAMILY TYPE

What was your family like when you were growing up, and what is it like now? The family is probably our strongest influence during our early life, showing us how people relate to each other, which values are most important, how broad—or narrow—our horizons can be, what we can expect from others, and how much autonomy we can expect to have. Although each family is as different and individual as its members, they fall into broad categories determined by the degree of closeness and the level of independence that is allowed. Identifying which type of family you belong to can help you understand how it functions and the ways it has affected you.

Looking for a healthy balance

All family types have their own specific benefits and drawbacks, but studies suggest that an open and supportive family is by far the best at maintaining a healthy balance of closeness, combined with respect for the needs of individual members and encouragement about exercising their autonomy. Many families, however, include characteristics of more than one type.

Your family responses

Read through the following four scenarios, and pick the response that comes closest to how your own family would act in each given situation. Then check your responses against the different conclusions set out below.

Paul feels disappointed when he fails some of his key school exams. When he tells his parents:

1. They tell him they don't think any less of him because of his failure, perhaps the papers weren't fair, and they encourage him to retake them, reassuring him that he shouldn't worry at all.

2. They commiserate but ask him to consider whether he is certain that he had really worked hard enough and to think about the best course of action to take now.

3. They are angry and disappointed in him, saying that he has wasted all of their time and not lived up to their expectations.

4. They make no comment, except to say that he might not be able to pursue his career if he fails his exams again.

LEVELS OF SUPPORT

Mostly ones—close and smothering

A warm, close, and supportive family can also be suffocating at times. There may be a strong sense of family loyalty but insufficient privacy or respect for developing independence. It may leave children unprepared for the less caring world outside.

Mostly twos—open and supportive

In this type of family, open discussion and respect for individual views fosters mutual support balanced by a degree of independence. The family may seem chaotic or brusque, but children nonetheless feel secure in the family's support while developing their autonomy.

Jonie, 19, has the chance of spending one year of her college course abroad. She is excited but nervous about being far from home. Her parents' response is:

1. They're proud that she has been "specially chosen," but are concerned that she'll be homesick once she gets there and that they won't be able to manage at home without her.

2. They congratulate her and suggest that she finds out as much as she possibly can about where she'll be studying and staying so that she feels well prepared and confident.

3. They are gratified but express doubts that she'll be able to handle the strain of living away from home. They decide to speak to her supervisor directly to find out if the college abroad will be a suitable environment for her.

4. They say she can go away if she likes, though they can't see why she can't just do her course here. If she is going, they ask her to shift her things up to the loft so that they can let her bedroom while she's away.

The family dog has died while the children were at school. The parents handle this situation by:

1. Gathering the children together and saying that the dog has "gone to Heaven."

2. Telling the children that the dog has died, and allowing them to see and touch it if they choose.

3. Informing the children that the dog has "gone away" and refusing to discuss the matter further.

4. Mentioning in passing that the dog has died, but avoiding discussing it, saying that they may get another one at some time in the future.

Lucy, aged 11, returns home from school with a letter asking for parental permission to allow her to attend sex education classes. The family decide:

1. To ask Lucy what she wants to do.

2. Lucy should attend the class, although they are already used to answering her questions openly.

3. Lucy should certainly not be exposed to such a subject at her age. They refuse permission and write to the school to complain.

4. They aren't very bothered either way, but check with other parents to see if any of them are letting their children attend the classes.

Mostly threes—autocratic and controlling

In an autocratic family, ideals are valued more highly than individual needs. The strong sense of structure is usually consistent, so children feel secure, but they may find it hard to express themselves, particularly if they want to do something not sanctioned by the family.

Mostly fours—distant and neglectful

This kind of family fosters self-reliance, but may neglect the emotional needs of its members. Openly displaying feelings may be seen as a loss of control. The lack of engagement can make it hard for children to show feelings or ask for what they need.

EARLY BUILDING BLOCKS

A S AN ADULT, you may believe that any decisions you make are based upon your ability to perceive different situations in a rational way. You might also think that this is very different from the kind of thinking you did as a child, and that you have somehow "grown out" of the influences you were under when small. In fact, much of the way we behave is determined by our childhood influences—particularly by how we saw adults behave within our own families.

First needs

Human beings have basic needs for food and protection, but they also have a strong craving for affection and intimacy. From earliest childhood, we establish an emotional bond with our parents, whose behavior may have a formative influence on our character. For example, separation from the mother (or other main carer) can cause children to feel insecure. Long-term separation can cause deeper problems, which may be reflected in later life. John Bowlby, an expert in childhood influences, showed through his studies that children behave in certain predictable ways when cut off from familiar loved ones. Although they may pass through stages of obvious distress and anger to apparently "normal" behavior, they may remain deeply damaged by these events as adults. They may find it difficult to believe they are lovable and wanted, and may develop a tendency to keep others at an emotional "arm's length,"

Childhood influences
From the moment we are born, we are influenced by both immediate family members and the generations that have gone before.

46

or to form repeated short-term relationships. Or they may later act out angry and violent feelings toward partners or friends because they have been unable to express their anger in other ways. Many people are unaware of the effect of their primal influences, seeing them as their own innate personality, and therefore immutable.

Repeated patterns

Fortunately, extreme neglect of children is still unusual. Most of us are shaped by less traumatic happenings, and by subtle messages from our adult carers about how we should think and act. How often your mother was cuddled and praised as a child may partially determine how much affection you are shown. If her family were not demonstrative, she may feel vaguely uncomfortable at showing her feelings toward you, or positively believe that "too much praise will make you big-headed." Alternatively, you may have been admired for almost everything you did as a child, and so find it hard to cope with criticism in later life.

Learning by example

Some types of behavior learned in childhood are passed on because the parents have acquired a set of beliefs from their own parents, and never questioned whether they were relevant to their own children. For instance, the child whose parents have grown up in a poor family may learn that every penny must be spent carefully even though his or her parents may not be consciously worried about money. This learning may not be taught in the traditional sense but by observation. For example, the child may notice that his father always counts his change carefully, that his mother always encourages him to choose inexpensive sweets, and that parental arguments are usually about money. These observations become part of the child's understanding about how money is handled and go on to become part of his or her own ethics and value system. Consequently, the child grows up feeling that he or she should be careful about money.

Breaking the mold

Challenges to these belief systems often occur during the teens, when adolescents tend to rebel against family standards as they strive to establish

TRIGGERS FROM THE PAST

Family get-togethers can often trigger old conflicts and jealousies as adult children regress to their childhood roles within the family hierarchy.

To overcome behavior patterns rooted in the past, you need to be aware of them and how they came about. For example, Jean dreads family get-togethers because she always gets stuck in the kitchen. As a young girl, she started overcompensating in the kitchen to compete with her sister, who was good at school. Jean knows she is now a success, but at her parents' house she still feels she has to prove herself by helping out. Moaning about a family dinner to a friend helped her realize how silly the situation was. So she rang her sister to discuss making the meal a treat for their mother, with each of them taking one course. The meal was a success and broke the established routine. From now on, when a family meal is planned, both daughters are involved on an equal basis when discussing the food arrangements.

their own sense of identity. Despite this early rebellion, however, many people find themselves re-enacting their parents' beliefs as they mature and go on to have families of their own.

British child psychologist D. W. Winnicott suggested that babies need parenting that responds to their individual needs, rather than rigid rulings. In other words, the child and the parent need to be tuned to each other in a complementary, yet ultimately flexible, way. Winnicott believed that the child who is encouraged to explore his or her personal potential, while at the same time being helped by his or her parents to understand the need for the care and love of others, is likely to enter into fulfilling relationships as an adult, and in turn, be able to pass on this sense of security to his or her own children.

CHANGING FAMILY PATTERNS

Difficult family situations often arise because individuals act or react in habitual, but not necessarily appropriate, ways, as the scenarios on these pages show. For example, a man may find he makes the decisions, while his wife takes a back seat. Falling into these familiar patterns may feel safe, but it inhibits your capacity to improve your relationships. It can also make you frustrated when you feel the need to change, but are hampered by your family's—and your own—expectations.

Countering interference

Some parents interfere too much in their adult children's lives; as the children struggle to be separate, conflict is almost inevitable.

At 34, John and his wife, Diane, have a small baby, and his parents are interfering, continuing a pattern of being over-controlling. John finds it hard to stand up to them. He could say, "I'm pleased that you take such an interest in your grandson, and I know you love him, but we have to work out how to raise him—mistakes and all—so please wait until we ask before you offer us advice."

Stuck in a groove
Families can become trapped in set patterns of behavior, so they act in habitual ways instead of finding the most appropriate response to each situation.

Stopping self-sacrifice

A common problem for those caught in difficult family issues is a feeling of being forced into self-sacrifice for the sake of others' needs or desires.

When Sarah's elderly mother falls ill just as Sarah is about to take her much-needed summer vacation, Sarah finds herself feeling angry and resentful. She feels torn between her desire to go, and the feeling that, as she has cared for her mother twice before, she will undoubtedly be expected to do so again. She feels isolated and trapped by her own past unselfishness, but also guilty and embarrassed that she is feeling so resentful.

Sarah could help herself by thinking more creatively about her mother's situation. She could certainly consider asking her brother to help out this time, or seek out short-term residential care. Sarah's belief that only she can handle the problem could also deny her mother any choices she may have wished to make over her care.

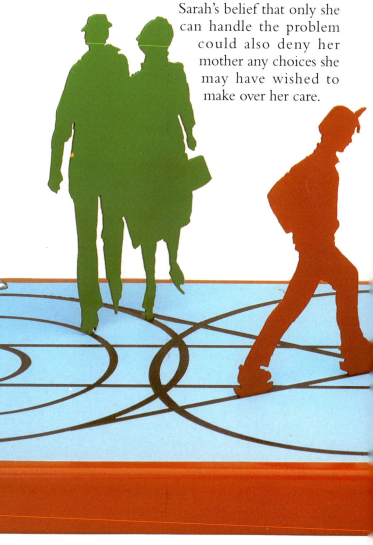

Fear of change

Anxiety about branching out into a different area can make people blame others for their own difficulties in changing.

Barbara has wanted to study French for some time, but is privately nervous about returning to college after 20 years. She has told her husband and teenage children of her wish, and they have encouraged her to try the course at her local college. However, she blames them for stopping her, implying that, although they encourage her, she still has to do the chores, so she cannot attend.

Barbara is unable to allow herself to follow the path she wants because of her underlying fear that she might find it too difficult, so it is easier to give herself an excuse rather than risk failure. She could decide to attend the course, and then tackle the practical problems. The family could get together and draw up a rota of tasks so that everyone is helping to run the household. To calm her nerves, Barbara could arrange a meeting with the college lecturer to discuss the course in advance to check that it will be stimulating and challenging but not too daunting.

Finding a new balance

In families where one parent gets landed with handling discipline, this can cause resentment and drive a rift between partners. Jim has always been the authority figure in his family, partly because his own father left when he was small and he became the "man of the house." His wife pressures him to take a stern line with their teenaged son, who has problems at school, but Jim wants to build a greater understanding with him. Jim could talk to his wife about establishing a joint approach to discipline as this will also be less confusing for their son. They need to create an atmosphere in which their son can talk about his problems.

The way ahead

Changing family relationships can be difficult but extremely rewarding. Tackling problems without resorting to manipulation or self-sacrifice makes people freer to be themselves, express their own needs and desires, and follow their own particular path; they can also give strong mutual support without needing to control each other.

JOB SATISFACTION

HOW MANY PEOPLE can honestly say that they actively love and enjoy their job? Surveys suggest that people who are truly happy with their working lives are in the minority. One of the reasons for this may be that, in spite of the strong link between career and self-image, in truth we rarely choose our own careers. A survey in the U.S. magazine *Psychology Today* revealed that as much as 40 percent of the population drifted into a career, irrespective of their background or specific education. Less than a quarter (23 percent) claimed to have chosen a career.

Given that most people spend the greater part of each day preparing for, traveling to, and doing a job that they find, at best, unsatisfying, and, at worst, a source of stress and unhappiness, finding a way to improve the quality of our working life is imperative. Fortunately, there are ways in which we can maximize our level of job fulfillment. For example, you can work on improving your current job, streamlining your workload (see "Effective Time Management" on pages 56-57), so that you have extra time to focus on the more interesting aspects of what you do. Or you may need to iron out difficulties with co-workers (see in particular "Can You Cope with Authority?" on pages 54-55, "Power Games" on pages 108-109, and "Are You Assertive?" on pages 112-113.)

Failing this, going for another job may be an option to consider, or perhaps even making a complete change of direction to a career that feels more in tune with you and what you have to offer.

Making the change

For many people contemplating a career change, the question is, "What job, where?" If you don't have a clear idea of what your next step should be, a practical self-help manual on job hunting and career changing such as *What Color is Your Parachute?* by Richard Nelson Bolles can help you to decide. Look realistically at what transferable skills you possess. Which of your skills—discovering, perceiving, talking, writing, etc—do you enjoy using most? What general areas of work—for

Time for change
Changing career has become a common occurrence as more people search for personal fulfillment in their work.

example banking, photography, publishing, and so on—interest you? Consider also the importance of the working environment, the end product, the hours, salary, what any given job actually entails, and what sort of equipment you would use or handle—which of these matter to you the most? Remember, too, that your attitude to work may alter as you mature: Research has shown that issues such as creativity, job satisfaction, and self-determination become much more important as we get older. Time also tends to mellow the need to prove ourselves, or to achieve success for its own sake.

Lateral moves

A sideways career move—one that either transfers your favorite skills into a new field of interest, or requires developing new skills in a field you are already working in and enjoy—is probably one of the most effective ways to change direction. For example, Julia, a disillusioned math teacher who wanted a change, identified that her strongest skills were a head for figures, communicating, assigning

tasks and monitoring, and self-motivation. She decided to take these skills to an area that interested her very much—the catering business. She approached a busy restaurateur, who took her on as his assistant responsible for day-to-day bookkeeping, buying in supplies, bookings, and overseeing the serving staff. Although Julia was operating in an entirely new work set-up, she was still drawing on many familiar skills that she genuinely enjoyed using, while also giving herself the opportunity to explore new possibilities. In Julia's case, she started helping out in the kitchen and discovered that she loved, and had a natural flair for, cooking. Eventually, she went on a part-time cookery course, became a chef, and later still, opened a restaurant.

ARE YOU IN THE RIGHT JOB?

We all feel a certain amount of dissatisfaction with our job—but for some people this can be a permanent state of affairs. You may think that enjoying work is a luxury, especially in a recession. However, you spend so much time at work that it is worth being as fulfilled as possible. This questionnaire will help you assess your level of satisfaction, and perhaps point the way to change—not necessarily a new job, maybe just a change of department or a shift of responsibilities. Score two points for **a**; one for **b**; none for **c**.

1. How do you feel generally about work?
a) Even if it's not the perfect job, I try to put as much of myself into it as possible.
b) It's alright—but I always feel it could be better.
c) It's just something I have to do to pay the bills.

2. What's your general attitude when you start looking for a job?
a) I have a clear idea what I'm looking for, but try to keep an open mind—there may be jobs out there that I've never thought of before.
b) I pretty much know what I'm looking for, and I just stick to that.
c) I take whatever's going—I can look for something else later.

The rules of the game
Finding the right job can seem like a complicated game. As far as possible, match the job to your individual personality and skills in order to make the pieces fit perfectly.

3. What's your attitude toward job interviews?
a) I make sure I'm really well-prepared, even if it's not my ideal job, and try to find out as much as possible.
b) I usually prepare well, but I hate them and often forget to ask important questions.
c) I do my best, but half the time, they've already given the job to someone inside the company, or a friend or relation of the boss.

4. How do you feel generally about the job you have at the moment?
a) I find it rewarding.
b) I get along OK—"better the devil you know."
c) It's just a job, so I shouldn't expect very much.

5. Do you take time out to think about your specific likes, dislikes, and skills?
a) Yes—I've sat down and made a written list, and every so often I revise it.
b) I'm pretty certain about what I like and what I'm good at—I don't really need to give it much thought.
c) How many people can find the ideal job for them?

6. Think about the things you like doing best in life, such as being with people. Is this a part of your job?
a) Very much so—that's partly why I've stayed here.
b) Not really, but work is more about skills, isn't it?
c) I don't think that you go to work to enjoy yourself.

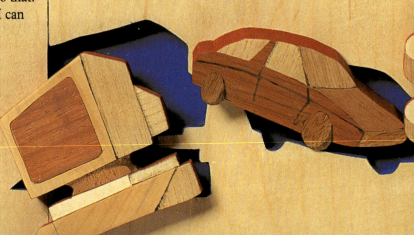

7. Think carefully about your main skills, such as "working quickly and accurately." Are you using them in your current job?
a) Most of the time.
b) Quite often, but I keep getting side-tracked into taking on tasks that I'm not so well suited to.
c) Very rarely—in fact, come to think of it, I'm not that sure what my skills are.

8. Have you recently taken any steps to acquire additional job skills?
a) Yes—I've been to evening classes/on-the-job training sessions.
b) I did some course ages ago, but basically, I just plod along.
c) No. Courses are a waste of time—either you can do the job or you can't.

9. How do you think your work fits in with the rest of your life?
a) Pretty well. I've learned quite a lot about myself personally through my work and sometimes I've even managed to make use of some of my outside hobbies and interests, too.
b) My job always seems to be taking over my personal life, even though I try to cut down my working hours.
c) It doesn't. My job is just something I do. I like to get it over with and get on with the rest of my life.

10. Do you think about what job you'll be doing a few years from now?
a) Yes—I've got several alternative plans for what I'd like to be doing and how I can achieve this.
b) Perhaps I'll get a promotion if I stay in my current job for a few more years—if I put in the time, I should be rewarded.
c) I try not to. I just keep my head down and hope for the best.

11. Why are you staying in your job?
a) I like it/I'm not—I'm looking elsewhere.
b) It's OK, and it's difficult to change.
c) I'd like to change, but I doubt that I'd get anything better.

12. Have you considered a major job change?
a) Yes—and I've even looked into special training/grants/moving house.
b) I think about it sometimes, but there's plenty of time for that....
c) No—once you're in one line of work, it's impossible to switch to another, isn't it?

How did you score?

0–5 points You have become pretty cynical, which can only hold you back. Even if jobs are scarce, it is worth trying to find a job or an aspect of your work that uses your unique skills and the things you like to do.
6–17 points You're getting there. You try to make sure you're in roughly the right job for you, but resist re-evaluating the situation every so often, and tend to get caught up in a daily grind. Don't feel guilty about enjoying yourself at work—it is allowed!
18–24 points You know that it is vital to analyze your skills and the things you enjoy and marry them up to your work. Your enthusiasm will open doors, so that even in a less-than-perfect job, you may find a fulfilling niche.

CAN YOU COPE WITH AUTHORITY?

Why do so many of us have ambivalent feelings toward figures in authority? Clearly, if a boss or manager is taking advantage of his or her position to play mindless power games with subordinates, it is normal and healthy to feel angry, even mutinous, at such abusive behavior. But how do you react when a perfectly reasonable request or suggestion is made by a supervisor? Do you find yourself, for example, answering back, and generally acting in a defiant manner; or do you instantly demur, but then find yourself procrastinating, losing paperwork, and engaging in other self-defeating activities?

Both types of behavior—openly aggressive and passively aggressive—are signs that you may have a problem with authority, and in both cases the difficulty may be traced back to childhood.

Authority and the family

In *Families and How to Survive Them*, Robin Skynner and John Cleese stress the importance of parents giving their children firm guidelines in terms of discipline and clear boundaries. These allow the child to develop a realistic view of the world—the family—and his or her place in it, and a safe environment in which to experience the extremes of his or her emotions and learn how to control them. Later on, the adult will know how to be an effective team member, while still retaining a strong sense of self-worth.

So what happens if the parents are either manipulative and controlling on the one hand, or over-indulgent and unable to set boundaries on the other? In the first case, the child may grow up to be timid, complying, and fearful of abandonment. And in the second, the child may turn into an adult who is constantly kicking against everything, forever the rebellious teenager.

On equal terms
The stronger our own sense of self-worth, the better we can relate to authority figures.

Skynner and Cleese call these two types the robot and the brat. Although they look very different on the outside, from the inside they share some similarities. Both cling to the fantasy that they are in some way different from everyone else, both find it hard to be part of a team, and both have unresolved issues regarding authority.

Don't tell me what to do

Take Alan, for example, who worked in the contracts department for a big company. Although he seemed conscientious and methodical, he was also a source of irritation and frustration to all those around him. His passive-aggressive behavior to authority took the form of a go-slow. He insisted that procedures were followed to the letter, and he took far longer than anyone else over paperwork—everyone assumed this meant he was being meticulous over the details, and this was the reason he gave when quizzed over his lack of progress. And yet, despite all Alan's apparent thoroughness, his supervisor was puzzled by the number of difficulties and delays associated with Alan's work.

Sally, on the other hand, was considered early on to be very good at her job in sales, but her general demeanor at work was a source of concern to her manager. She was often late for meetings, for example, and made the assumption that, as she was a bit of a star, she could create her own rules. Whenever her manager wanted to discuss her progress or make suggestions as part of an ongoing assessment program, Sally became defensive, and quickly went on the attack. Her behavior to her co-workers was distant and condescending.

Resolving inner conflicts

Although both Alan and Sally's attitudes to authority manifested themselves in very different ways, their behavior was caused by a deep insecurity that stemmed from childhood. Brought up in families where basic parental messages on self-control and self-worth were distorted, both had formed very early on the belief that they were somehow

DON'T BLOW A FUSE

Here are a series of points that may help you to deal with authority calmly and effectively. Remember, the bottom line is that if you are unhappy with your employer, you can always seek another. But also ask yourself whether, to some extent, it is *you* who has a problem with authority. Check it out with your colleagues—if you're the only one who thinks your boss is the manager from hell, this is a sign to rethink your attitude.

• Don't lose your head. However satisfying you might find screaming at your boss in the short term, it rarely serves any useful purpose, and it is unprofessional behavior.

• Relax and count to ten! Although this is something of a cliché, it can work. If you feel yourself overwhelmingly losing control, use this device as a way to defuse yourself.

• If you feel you are being bullied or badly treated, think about the situation rationally. Sit down with your boss and discuss the matter—the chances are that he or she is unaware of the problem. If you get nowhere with your boss, go further up the line, or perhaps to the personnel manager. Whatever you do, don't suffer in silence—that guarantees that nothing will be sorted out.

• If your feelings of resentment become too great, ask yourself what is going on. If you discover that the real problem is that your current job is not for you, do something about it. Don't make life so difficult for yourself in the office that your employer is forced to make the decision to leave for you. On the other hand, if you sense you are kicking against authority for its own sake, consider getting some help, such as seeing a counselor or therapist.

unworthy of affection or attention. Sally's response was to act as badly as she felt—behavior that got her noticed, although the attention she received was often critical or negative. To win approval, Alan had developed a slightly different coping strategy. He tried very hard to conform and at the same time unconsciously sabotaged all his efforts to be a "good boy," to fit in and be accepted.

Without some adjustments on the part of Alan and Sally, their situations could only get worse. For Alan, it was not until his supervisor gave him a formal warning, and a work colleague took the trouble to draw his attention to his passive-aggressive behavior, that he realized that he needed to look more closely at the part he was playing in making his working life so difficult. When Sally was dismissed for swearing at a client and losing a major sale, only then could she acknowledge that she had a problem, and that if she didn't do something about it, her promising career was in jeopardy.

EFFECTIVE TIME MANAGEMENT

Companies have spent a great deal of time and money looking at the way in which people work. Research has suggested that improving time management skills can make employees up to 50 percent more effective, advice which can be applied to both work and leisure activities. It doesn't mean that people work harder, merely that better organization allows them to get more done. One of the ways to use time most effectively is to have a clear sense of your goals in life.

We discussed how to set goals on pages 20-21, but remember, once you have set your goals, they need to be continually re-assessed. How else will you know if you are on course? The U.S. engineer Buckminster Fuller likened this process to controlling the rudder of a boat—getting to the destination is not about holding the rudder firm, setting the course, and then leaving the boat to get there; there need to be many adjustments made along the way.

Avoid interruptions

One of the most effective ways of losing time is through interruptions; the average day is full of distractions that divert you from your goals. For example, a telephone ringing may demand your attention urgently because it is making a loud noise right under your nose. It demands that you respond *immediately*. But while some calls are important, others are completely trivial. If the call is not important, you should explain to the caller that this is not a good moment to talk and arrange to ring him or her back later. If possible, before you become engaged in an important task, arrange for someone else to answer the telephone, or use an answering machine. When it comes to making telephone calls, map out a time to make them all at once. That way, you will be able to concentrate on other things for longer periods, as your time and concentration will be less fragmented.

Interruptions from visitors can also be very time-consuming. Choose certain times when you do not want to be disturbed and make people who are likely to visit you aware of them. Unexpected visitors should be dealt with courteously but speedily. If necessary, schedule another time to see them. Once you have taken all the steps you can to deter others from distracting you, then you will be able to apply yourself to the tasks in hand.

Prioritize

In order to move as rapidly as possible toward your long-term goals, you will need to avoid activities that are simply time-wasting and learn how to prioritize effectively. Periodically, consider your long-term plan, break down each goal, and work out what you have to do to achieve it. Look at the measures you can take toward these goals in the short- and medium-term, then plan what you need to do on a daily basis.

Write a list of goals for each day and then put them in order of priority. Many people simply start working on the first item that needs attention. This haphazard approach can mean that important, but not urgent, matters are pushed to one side—tasks that might move you toward your long-term goals but do not have to be done this minute. For instance, it may be important to you to present a paper at a conference in two months time, but your urgent work is the papers you have to grade today. You have to ensure you do both. Also include leisure goals in your short- and medium-term lists. They may be less urgent than work goals, but they are just as important in the quest for a balanced, interesting, and meaningful life.

Climb the stairway to success
Efficient use of your time is necessary if you are to achieve all that you want in your life. These tips will cut down on wasted time and help you stay on top.

TIME TIPS

In order to reach your goals, it is necessary to make the best possible use of your time. That is not to say that your whole life should be structured, but it can be only too easy to fritter away time on trivia without leaving yourself time to do what you really want. Look at the tips on the right. They will help you increase your time management skills, and take you step by step toward all your goals.

Learn to prioritize
• Make a list and prioritize each task on it.
• Don't do the less important things first, just because they are easy.
• Stick to your list—resist the temptation to do things that are unscheduled.

Think of yourself
• Listen to your body. Try to schedule tasks for times when you are most alert mentally.
• Remember to schedule in regular breaks and time for yourself throughout the day. Periodic rests will help you to work more efficiently.

Know your goals
• Try to give at least a few moments' thought each day to your goals in the medium- and long-term.
• Make your daily tasks measurable. If you don't have an end result in mind, how will you know if you've been successful?
• Being active is not enough in itself. Look at the tasks on your list. Are they helping you achieve your goals?

Make plans
• The golden rule of time management is to plan out your day, in as much detail as possible.
• Make a written plan—diaries or forms broken down into hourly units are extremely good for this purpose.
• When you plan, make sure that you add contingency time—everything always takes much longer than you think.

Take action
• Don't leave tasks unfinished. If a job seems too big, break it down into smaller tasks.
• Be proactive. Deal with problems quickly.
• Get off on the right foot—make the first hour of the day count.
• Analyze your time and find out if there are any persistent time-wasting activities.
• Don't procrastinate. Putting off jobs that you dislike simply creates additional pressure and stress—and it won't make them go away, either.

Save time
• Keep your working environment well organized. You can save time simply by knowing where everything is.
• Make the most of dead time. Sort out minor matters whilst traveling.
• Know your own abilities. Plan your time and set yourself realistic deadlines. If you take on too much you may do all the tasks, but to a lower standard. If you are under pressure from others, learn to say no.

MANAGING RELATIONSHIPS

I F YOU ARE TRYING to find ways to lead a more fulfilled life, at some point the spotlight of your attention will fall on your various relationships—with family, lovers, friends, and colleagues. Relationships can bring great pleasure and satisfaction—when they work—and unhappiness when they don't. Understanding when your relationships are working well and taking steps to improve them when they are not is an important way of taking control of your life.

Letting in light

If you are in the dark about why your relationships are not satisfying you, pull back the curtains and take a good look at them in a clear light.

Basic ingredients

A relationship does not have to be perfect in order to work. However, all good relationships have the same basic ingredients.

Most importantly, in a happy relationship you are able to be who you really are, and you allow the other person to do the same. This means that you are comfortable to talk openly about the things that are important to you and are clear about how you wish to be treated. It also means that you respect that the other person is different from yourself, and that you do not seek to change them.

Having an understanding of the other person is another basic ingredient of a good relationship. It means that you know what is important to them and how they wish to be treated by you. Then if your relationship runs into problems, having understanding equips you to deal with difficulties.

No relationship can survive without commitment. This need not be a frightening concept. At its most basic it means putting energy and care into your relationships: planning get-togethers with friends; giving time to your children; visiting elderly relatives; having time on your own with your partner.

Communicate effectively

A fundamental way in which your relationship exhibits these basic ingredients is in your ability to communicate effectively with each other. Communication involves both talking honestly and listening attentively. This means voicing your appreciation of the other person in terms of your love and affection for them. It also means finding a way to air your difficulties and frustrations—and your needs—however difficult this might be. And, of course, it means listening to and respecting the other person's thoughts and feelings, too.

If you find yourself avoiding initiating difficult conversations, ask yourself why. Are you afraid that either one of you might get upset or angry? If this is the case, it may well be that the problems in your relationship have been allowed to fester rather than be expressed and cleared up. Anger is difficult for everyone, but suppressing it can make matters much worse. It can be almost impossible to have an honest and loving relationship when both parties are too busy trying to avoid getting either angry or upset.

Taking responsibility

An inability to take responsibility, and a tendency to blame others, undermine a relationship. They are a sign that you are not communicating, do not understand the other person, and that you are not putting energy into the relationship. A successful relationship is one in which two individuals meet on equal terms, taking responsibility for themselves and for the relationship. For many people, however, taking responsibility is difficult, particularly when it comes to accepting their own failings. In these cases, people commonly blame others for their own lack of success and happiness. For more on taking responsibility see pages 110–111.

Making changes

A relationship is like a car: it needs fuel to work. You fill up the tank in good times, and in tough times let it run low. When it runs out of fuel, it stops working. If your relationship is not working you can try to improve it or end it. Working through problems can strengthen a relationship. First, a decision to change the relationship is needed. Knowing how to make positive change is more difficult, however.

Many couples find it difficult to improve things on their own. There is no shame in this. Counselors are expert in guiding you to an understanding of the problems, and in pinpointing ways you can make positive change.

COMPATIBILITY MYTHS

Many people believe that in the best relationships the individuals see eye to eye on everything. This is rarely the case. Being compatible with someone essentially means getting on well together, of course, and sharing the same basic aims. This can, indeed, lead to a harmonious relationship, and some individuals naturally fall into step.

However, closeness does not necessitate sameness. Understanding and accepting the differences between you brings a richness to the relationship and allows you to learn more about yourself and the other person.

If you are concerned about areas of incompatibility, pinpoint where you are out of step and discuss them openly with the person involved. This will help you both to learn more about each other, and to discover acceptable compromises.

Precious pearl
Just as a piece of grit becomes a pearl, a certain amount of friction can become a positive feature.

RELATIONSHIPS AND DEPENDENCY

In all relationships, a certain amount of mutual dependency is normal and healthy. Our need to be comforted and nurtured by another person, to be made love to, to be supported in times of stress, and to be listened to, is an intrinsic part of an intimate relationship.

Obviously, people vary in their need to rely on others according to their age, personality, and circumstances, and there is no cut-and-dried definition of how much dependence is healthy. What is more indicative of a well-balanced relationship is the quality of the dependency, rather than the extent. For instance, the fact that a couple always goes out together may simply mean they have mutual friends. But it might also be a way of relating in an over-dependent way—not wanting to be excluded from any of the other's experiences.

The ideal relationships are interdependent, those in which both parties can rely on the other for the fulfillment of some of their needs, some of the time, while not relinquishing their independence or denying responsibility for their own lives.

very idea that there are people in the world who can be relied on seems a fantasy. Peter, for example, has a problem depending on others. At first glance he appears to be the very picture of independence and self-reliance, taking great pride in being a shoulder to cry on for his less self-sufficient partners. He loves to cook and care for them when they are unwell, but finds it difficult to allow his partners to look after him. When his latest girlfriend, Kathy, whom he really hoped would be a partner for life, threatened to leave because she felt

Hiding from ourselves

For some people, the word dependency does not conjure up positive associations. For them, the associations are negative, bringing to mind times when they have felt humiliated or rejected when asking for help. Their experience of dependency has been so tied up with loss and disappointment that they cannot allow themselves to be vulnerable again. This is particularly true of people whose parents abused or abandoned them at an early age, or if one or both parents died. Similarly, to people who have had no experience of anyone being sensitive to their needs, the

A careful balance
In healthy relationships, partners are able to depend on each other to share their needs and fears, while not forgetting that they are individually responsible for their own lives.

she couldn't get close to him, he was forced to examine his feelings. He realized that he was still haunted by the despair he felt when his wife had left him some years previously, which in turn echoed his feelings when his mother had walked out of the family home. At both times he had felt utterly helpless and abandoned, and as a result he created for himself situations in which, by not allowing himself to depend on others, those feelings would not arise. Peter discussed this with Kathy, and this act in itself made her feel closer to him. He, in turn, realized that her love need not threaten his independence.

At the other extreme are people who had their dependency needs met too perfectly in childhood, and who have fallen into the trap of expecting others to anticipate their needs without having to ask for what they want. Such people are destined to feel forever let down because they do not realize that their demands are unreasonable.

The dependency trap

Over-dependency is equally a problem, as we have all seen in relationships in which one partner seems to have no independent existence at all. Marion and Bill were such a couple. After Marion had a collision in the car, her husband forbade her to drive alone. Friends were outraged at the curtailment of her freedom, but Marion was privately pleased that she would have more of Bill's time, and he was satisfied that his wife needed him.

While the two may be happy in these roles at present, it is not a healthy situation. Both are stifled by the dependency. Furthermore, although the dependency may appear to create a strong bond between them, their relationship is, in fact, particularly vulnerable. Any change in circumstances or emotion will automatically threaten the position of the other person. We look more closely at some of the reasons for dependency problems on pages 62-63, and suggest how to help to overcome them.

ARE YOU AN INDEPENDENT ADULT?

In childhood, we depend on parents or carers for our health and happiness. If, as adults, we allow ourselves to depend on another, we sometimes revert to childlike responses. To help you spot whether this is happening in your relationships, look at the two responses listed below that first express the immature reaction of an over-dependent adult, and then the way that an independent adult might respond. Do you ever find yourself reacting in a way that is similar to the immature response?

Immature adult
An immature adult cannot easily identify his/her own needs:
"Can't you see I'm miserable? Why aren't you being more sympathetic?"

An immature adult expects someone else to provide for him/her:
"I really want a car, perhaps if I work on dad he'll buy me one."

An immature adult finds it difficult to deal with frustration:
"I want a hug now!"

Mature adult
A mature adult is responsible for his/her own needs:
"I feel really tired and irritable— perhaps I need a break."

A mature adult is able to provide for him/her self:
"If I want a car, I need a part-time job."

A mature adult is able to contain his/her frustration:
"Pity Sally doesn't want to make love tonight. Guess she'll feel better in a few days."

SIGNS OF OVER-DEPENDENCE

When we feel low or lost in the world, it can be so easy to look to other people to boost our self-esteem, to give us direction, to heal our wounds, or at least to dull the pain. To some extent we are all over-dependent on others at times, but it can become a way of life, and a means of avoiding dealing with our own problems and taking responsibility for our lives.

In its most obvious form, over-dependence may mean looking to another person to answer your needs. In much more extreme cases—referred to as co-dependent relationships—dependence on another may extend to putting that person's well-being above your own. People with this level of dependency deliberately seek friends and partners who need straightening out and looking after—even those with serious problems such as alcoholism or drug addiction. This kind of relationship is looked at in more detail on pages 64-65.

Below we have identified some different factors that can lead to dependency problems in relationships. If you recognize any of the emotions described, you might benefit from tackling the exercises that follow each section. They are designed to help you think further about the nature of your relationships with other people.

Low self-esteem

Our self-esteem can take a sharp nosedive after periods of extreme difficulty and stress, such as a divorce or unemployment. Or it may be that we have never really had a strong belief in our own abilities and good qualities. Either way, it is during these times of great vulnerability that we turn to outside sources to re-affirm our self-belief.

Useful exercises

• Write a list of things that you don't like about yourself and then things that you do like: Which list is longer? Do you think that the two lists are a fair reflection of your character?

• Think of three things that are going well in your life. Did you make them happen? How important were other people in making them happen?

Don't leave me
Sometimes life can seem too difficult for us to handle on our own and we look to other people to sort out all our problems.

Lack of self-validation

When people are extremely unsure of themselves, they may depend on someone else to tell them who they ought to be. But this means that we are simply trying to please important people in our lives. An example of this is the "company man" who works excruciatingly hard to meet work targets and please his boss. If you are motivated solely by a desire to become the sort of person that your lover, partner, parent, or boss wants you to be (often more in their interests than your own), the performance can take you over at the expense of your autonomy.

Useful exercise

• Can you think of an occasion when you have given someone the response they wanted to hear simply in order to make you feel better about yourself? How did you feel when you did this? Write down at least three reasons why you think you acted that way.

Stand tall
A happy relationship comes from recognizing that you are independent and have your own needs, separate from those of your partner.

No needs and no wants

Another characteristic of the over-dependent relationship is that one or both partners are unaware of their own needs. This may happen when adults lapse into childhood patterns and expect others to take care of them, often without feeling that they have to say what it is they need or want. Another possible way to avoid dealing with one's own needs is to look after someone else so well that you simply don't have any time left to look to yourself. This might appear like generosity, but it can often be a cover-up, masking very strong emotions that feel too frightening to be released.

Useful exercise

• Write down at least three things that you would like to achieve in your life: What are the obstacles that are preventing you from achieving them? Do you feel you are using your responsibilities to other people as one of the obstacles?

Less than you deserve

Perhaps the most damaging result of low self-esteem is that you feel you are in some way bad or undeserving. You expect very little from the world, and put up with a lot—including inferior relationships. Furthermore, you may find yourself depending on people whose behavior is exploitative or selfish because you do not believe that you are worth respecting and valuing. And you probably find that you have surrounded yourself with others who reflect your own lowly view of yourself. This vicious circle makes it more difficult to break out of unrewarding relationships because you really don't believe you deserve better.

Useful exercises

• Write down five statements about how you expect to be treated, and five statements about how you feel you should treat others. Examine the way one of your close friends treats you. Does their behavior meet these expectations?

• Describe a time when you were treated badly. How did it feel? How did you respond?

Confused boundaries

People who become involved in over-dependent relationships are often less able to see themselves as separate from those to whom they are emotionally attached. This means they lose a sense of their own and other people's personal boundaries. Having reasonably intact boundaries protects us from various sorts of abusive behavior. For example, we are instantly aware when someone gets too close to us sexually. But more everyday examples of not respecting others' boundaries include reading a spouse's letter, or walking into a teenager's bedroom before knocking on the door. People can invade each other emotionally, too, by criticizing, judging, mocking, or playing on another's vulnerabilities.

Useful exercises

• Describe an occasion in which you have overstepped the mark in a relationship. Describe an occasion in which you feel others have done this to you.

• Think about the relationships you have with these people—why do you think these incidents occurred with these particular individuals?

THE CO-DEPENDENCY TRAP

At what point does a relationship stop being over-dependent and become co-dependent? Most experts agree that it is a question of degree. In the classic co-dependent relationship, one partner is addicted to something—whether it's to alcohol, drugs, work, gambling, or sex. Both partners suffer deeply from all the insecurities and low self-esteem already described on pages 62–63. While the partners in over-dependent relationships may show aspects of being victim and caretaker or "rescuer," in a co-dependent relationship this is the very basis of the way in which two people operate together. Co-dependency may manifest itself as intense and destructive emotional reactions in the "rescuing" person, outbursts over which he or she appears to have no control, and that are blamed on the person he or she is trying to please.

Co-dependency and addiction

People who repeatedly seem to choose partners and friends who need long-term looking after, whether they need drying out or sorting out, have fallen into the co-dependency trap. From the outside looking in it can be baffling to understand why and how these relationships endure. People who are addicted to drugs or alcohol, in spite of heartfelt protestations that they could give up if they chose, almost never give up their habit spontaneously, unless they are prepared to admit the extent of their problem to themselves and seek professional help. Sometimes their relatives and partners get drawn into the battle for control. For instance, if a husband is addicted to alcohol or drugs, his wife gets addicted in turn to both controlling and covering up her

Pas de deux
It takes two to live out a co-dependent relationship, each partner playing and exchanging roles to fuel the dependency.

partner's habit. Then, further along the line, the co-dependent pattern often repeats itself when the wife's family or friends may try to control her, by encouraging her to leave her husband.

The myth of the rescuer

It can be very tempting for those living with addicts to think that they can rescue the addict from their condition, thereby giving them a new lease of life. The problem of rescuing is that it doesn't work—it simply reinforces the illusion that the addict does not have control over his or her life. Recovery is possible only when the addict finds the grain of strength that encourages him or her to begin to recognize the damage he or she is wreaking. Being rescued prevents that opportunity.

Those who live with addicts or alcoholics often find it very difficult to understand that not only do they play a part in the addiction, but that they themselves might also have a problem that needs attention. They have become blind to their own pain and to the emotional damage. Part of the recovery task for the co-dependent partner involves ceasing to hide from painful feelings that have been kept at bay for so long.

Taking control

Preventing yourself from rescuing someone close to you who may have become ill, penniless, or homeless as a result of his or her habit can feel heartless, but it is crucial to break the pattern of negative control—that is, to stop being controlled by another, and trying to control him or her. This type of negative behavior, which is discussed in the box, right, is known as "enabling." The first step toward this is to regain control of yourself, by cutting out the behavior that upholds the situation.

If you are involved with someone who is chemically addicted, you should both seek professional help as soon as possible. The best results are achieved when both partners, or all the family, join a recovery program. This is because everyone concerned needs to be able to confront the problem, breaking down the denial and self-deception accompanying the addiction. They also need empathetic, non-judgmental support from others in the same boat while they begin the long and difficult task of regaining control of their lives.

Break free
Take hold of the strings that bind you to co-dependent behavior and release yourself from their grip.

OUT OF CONTROL?

Any behavior by a co-dependent partner which, by assuming responsibility for sorting out the other person's problem, prevents the addict from assuming proper responsibility for his or her own life is termed "enabling." In fact, the rescuer's tendency to abdicate self-control in favor of controlling the other person is thought to fuel his or her partner's addiction.

If you are living with someone who you suspect may have an addiction, it can be revealing to monitor how much of your life is given over to caretaking for them. If you answer Yes to most of the following questions, you may have adopted an enabling role.

Do you:

• Beg, demand, or insist that the habit be given up?
• Hide drink or drugs to keep him or her sober?
• Avoid situations or company in which your partner might be encouraged to indulge the habit?
• Take him or her home or clean up afterward when he or she gets drunk or high?
• Go through your partner's belongings to make sure he or she is "clean" and "straight?"
• Hide the extent of the addiction from everyone?
• Neglect your other relationships and interests in order to keep an eye on your partner?
• Become depressed or anxious because of his or her behavior?

CHAPTER THREE

KICK
THE HABIT

ARE YOU LIKE GULLIVER, unable to break free from your restraints to take control of your life? If so, your behavior may subconsciously be tying you down. Habits—as well as addictions, compulsions, and obsessions—creep into our lives so quietly that very often we don't know that they are there and are not aware of how much they are controlling us. It is only when we experience dissatisfaction with the way our life is progressing that we feel ourselves to be in the grip of a controlling force. This chapter invites you to analyze your habits, to judge if any are restricting or even damaging you, and to free yourself of them.

We start by defining what a habit is and how it differs from an addiction, a compulsion, and an obsession. These terms are often used interchangeably, but in fact relate to very different things. In essence, habits are a form of behavioral shorthand, a pattern that we use over and over; on the other hand, addictions, compulsions, and obsessions are things that we feel driven to do and are not able to contemplate stopping.

Quizzes and searching questions help you to identify your habitual behaviors and to work out for yourself whether they are positive or negative, or even

neutral time-fillers. The sections on pages 72-75 offer practical ways in which you can alter your behavior patterns.

Addictive behaviors are harder to recognize than habits—and harder to kick. We offer you encouragement to uncover addictions—whether to work, food, exercise, alcohol, or nicotine—and to understand what drives you to need them. "Get off the Hook," on pages 86-87 gives you practical suggestions for freeing yourself: how far you can go yourself, ways in which friends can help, and when you might want to seek help.

Perhaps, however, you don't feel in control of your life because you don't seem to develop happy love relationships. On pages 92-97 we explore the kinds of love addiction that can take over your relationships, invite you to discover whether you are hooked on love, and offer ways for you to break the cycle.

The chapter closes with an in-depth look at obsessions and compulsions, what causes them, and why they need to be taken in hand. It then offers practical strategies for curing them.

Whatever your kind of habitual behavior, this chapter gives you the confidence and practical support you need to break the ties that bind you.

IF HABITUAL PATTERNS OF BEHAVIOR SEEM TO BE CONTROLLING YOU,

TAKE THE OPPORTUNITY TO FREE YOURSELF FROM THEIR GRIP

AND TAKE CONTROL OF YOUR LIFE.

HABITUAL BEHAVIOR

BECAUSE THE WHOLE AREA of habits and addictions is very complex, psychiatrists define and classify the different types of normal and abnormal behavior. It is important to understand the difference between a habit and an addiction, otherwise you could decide you're addicted to something when you're not, and worry needlessly. On the other hand, you may well discover that you have developed one or more addictions without even being aware of it.

What's the difference?

Habit, addiction, obsession, compulsion —these four words are often used interchangeably, but actually mean very different things. Some confusion stems from the fact that the conditions the words describe often overlap, so that what starts out as a habit eventually becomes an addiction, for example.

In essence, a habit is a pattern of behavior or thinking that happens automatically. We are often quite unaware of our habits—we do them without thinking—and those around us can be just as unaware of them as we are.

A simple way to distinguish a habit from an addiction is whether you feel you have control over what you do. If you habitually do something, you could easily change it if you wanted to. However, if you are unable to resist it, you have lost your freedom to choose and have become addicted.

For some people, a habit stays a habit, and that's that. For others, a habit may become so necessary to their emotional well-being that it becomes an addiction. Ben was in the habit of having a

Are you hooked?

We are so much creatures of habit that it can be hard to know the difference between a habit and an addiction.

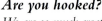

glass or two of wine with his meal in the evenings. It was a treat he gave himself after a hard day at the office. When the pressure began to build at work after his boss suddenly left, Ben began to have a glass of wine with his lunch in order to relax. One day he didn't have time to go to the pub and felt agitated all afternoon. Without being aware of what was happening, Ben was becoming addicted to something that had started as an enjoyable treat.

An addiction usually involves a physical and emotional dependency—smoking, eating, drinking, drug taking, or even taking exercise. Here, your body has learned to need a substance, which may provide emotional relief as well. Because the physical and emotional aspects of an addiction are strongly connected, it's usually impossible to treat one without treating the other.

Habits may be acceptable or unacceptable, and some addictions—to alcohol and nicotine, for example—are considered socially acceptable. This may give the person "permission" to indulge their addiction in the open. What the world often does not see, however, is the extent to which the habit or addiction controls the person's life. Other addictions—such as binge-eating or drug abuse—are socially unacceptable and usually kept hidden.

Compulsions and obsessions

Psychiatrists usefully differentiate between compulsions and obsessions, two terms that are often confused both one with the other and with habits and addictions. Very simply, a compulsion is a physical act—when someone feels compelled to look ten times before crossing the road, for example. Whereas a person may be unaware of their habits, somebody with a compulsion is frequently aware of their need—which is often desperate—to carry out a particular ritual.

The word "obsession" describes a person's thoughts and feelings: a persistent word, thought, or phrase that is repeated over and over. Sometimes obsessional thinking can lead to compulsive or addictive behavior. For example, a person may become addicted to alcohol or eating in order to drown out negative, painful thoughts and feelings. If a person suffers from feelings of obsessive love toward another, they may also find themselves acting out new patterns of behavior.

HABIT OR ADDICTION?

If your bad habits seem to be out of control, they may have become addictions. See whether any of the following apply to you.

• Do you smoke? How many a day, at what times?
• Do you regularly use any illegal drugs? How often do you use them?
• Do you drink alcohol? How much per week/day? Do you drink at particular times or in certain situations?
• Do you drink alone?
• Do you ever get drunk? How often?
• Do you take any prescribed medication such as tranquillizers, antidepressants, or sleeping pills? How long have you been taking them?
• Do you watch more TV/videos than you would like? For how many hours a day?
 • When you are feeling down, do you buy yourself things you do not need and cannot afford in order to cheer yourself up?
• Are you constantly overdrawn or in debt?
• Do you gamble?
• Do you tend to do particular things when you are upset, like eat, drink, or watch TV too much?
• Do you have problems controlling your eating?
• Do you tend to swing between the extremes of eating too much and dieting fanatically?
• Do you exercise even when you are sick?
• Have you ever inflicted an injury upon yourself?
• Do you always find yourself a victim in relationships?

Only you can decide

If you have answered Yes to any of these questions, then you may have the potential to become addicted. This does not mean you are headed for disaster as most of us do some of the above to a greater or lesser extent, particularly when feeling low or under increased pressure. You can tell you are addicted to a behavior when you are unable to stop doing it, even when you know its dangers.

WHAT ARE YOUR HABITS?

From the moment we get up until we go to bed, much of our everyday behavior consists of habits that we follow without thinking. Mostly, there is nothing wrong with that: People couldn't function effectively if they had to reconsider every activity. However, some kinds of habitual pattern can lead to situations that we would like to alter.

By uncovering your habits you gain a clear picture of how you behave. You can then decide which habits are beneficial and which unhelpful, and make efforts to change those with which you are uncomfortable.

Underlying emotions

It is important to understand your habits—what they are, when they arise, and why—because bad habits may be symptoms of underlying emotional difficulties. You can reveal any emotional problems by removing or stopping the habit, thus uncovering the source of anxiety or discomfort. Be aware that this may be a painful process.

For example, for as long as they could remember, Tony and Margaret always turned on the television after their evening meal. Margaret felt that they were not as close as they had once been, so one evening she suggested that instead of watching TV, they sit and talk. A long silence ensued, and the tension in the room grew and grew until Margaret turned on the set again. This confirmed her fears about the relationship.

In the end, Margaret found a less difficult occasion to discuss her concerns with Tony. Although he was reluctant at first to admit that they had grown apart, Tony eventually conceded that he and Margaret needed to open up a dialogue about their relationship and how they could improve matters.

Learned behavior

Your brain learns the sequence of habitual behavior patterns in the same way that it learns anything else: by repetition. It isn't able to judge independently whether something you do is good or bad.

The hidden agenda
Habits such as regularly watching TV or engaging in a hobby may serve to distract attention away from underlying, problematic issues.

If an activity is repeated enough times, it will become automatic, and you will do it without thinking. If you have a bad habit of slumping in your chair, for example, it will take a while before you are able to "retrain" your mind not to tell your body to slump as soon as you sit down.

Good and bad habits

Not every habit is a bad one: some are beneficial and others neutral—just filling in time. Everybody has a mixture of all three types. For instance, maybe you always leave for appointments with ten minutes to spare, in case there is heavy traffic. However, perhaps you hang around outside the door until the time of your appointment and then dash in, looking disorganized and rushed.

It is important to remember that your mind has learned a behavior that it will continue to repeat until you tell it to stop. Your challenge is to abandon any habits you do not want, and gain good ones with which to replace them.

THROUGH THE KEYHOLE

Do you know what your habits are? Are you aware of which ones are beneficial, which harmful, and which time-filling? Answer the following questions and use them as a springboard to examine other aspects of your habitual behavior.

• Do you always switch on the TV or radio when you come home?
• Do you automatically make yourself a coffee at set points during the day?
• Do you follow a set routine when you get up in the morning?
• Do you always carry an umbrella when you leave the house?
• Do you bite your nails?
• Do you always leave drink in your glass and food on the side of the plate?
• Do you constantly clear "tickles" from your throat?
• Do you find yourself using the same phrase over and over again?
• Do you always make sure that you have money in your purse?
• Do you drink a bottle of wine with every evening meal?
• Do you always end up going to bed later than you had intended?
• Do you clean the house on a particular day each week?

Assuming positive habits

While habits are automatic behaviors, this does not mean that we pick up habits purely at random. For example, saying thank you is a positive habit that we learned when we were small. As adults, we can continue to assume positive behaviors that enhance our lives. Think about the positive habits you would like to include in your behavior—try considering the habits of people you admire.

Once you have pinpointed two or three habits you would like to assume, think of opportunities for incorporating them into your day. Perhaps you would like to smile more often, for example. Watch yourself in a mirror while you practice, make sure that you smile naturally and in appropriate circumstances, and don't overuse the habit.

CHANGING YOUR HABITS

In order to change your habitual behavior you need to tell your brain over and over again what you want or don't want your body or mind to do. You need to reprogram yourself. First you need to become aware of the habits you wish to change. Don't try to change too many at once: You will find this difficult and will become easily disheartened. Instead, concentrate on one or two that you pinpointed in the exercise on pages 70-71.

After this, you need to observe your habit in action. Try to remain as detached as possible, as if you were watching another person. It's useful to repeat phrases like "Now I'm doing...," "Now I feel like...," which help you to understand your habit. This technique requires practice.

Assessing bad habits

Behavior therapy, developed in the 1950s and 1960s, helps people overcome self-defeating behaviors by learning about them and exchanging them for more positive patterns. A highly practical type of therapy, it aims not only to change bad habits but to instill positive ones in their place by the use of practice and repetition until they become natural.

One behavior therapy technique is keeping a diary of a habit, which enables you to assess what you're doing and thinking more clearly. Make the diary as detailed as possible—noting the activity, time, your mood, if you are alone, and where you are—and you will start to see a pattern emerge. For example, you might feel you "need" several cups of coffee at the start of the day. But your habits diary might reveal that you drink more coffee when you are expecting a tough day or as a way of avoiding tackling a particular task. This awareness of what triggers an unwanted habit may in itself be sufficient to bring about a change in people who are already highly motivated, and can use the trigger as a signal for self-control.

LINKED HABITS

You may find that in trying to change one habit, you have to change others that are linked to it. For example, Jill wanted to overcome her habit of being late for work. She thought that her difficulty lay in habitually forgetting to set her alarm clock. However, she discovered that even when she did remember, she would still be late. Eventually, Jill found that only by changing her getting-up routine so that she got dressed before having her coffee was she able to succeed.

Domino effect
You may have several habits in the way of your goal—alter these, and the end result should fall into place.

To change her routine, Jill stuck up pieces of paper to remind herself to set her clock, and also left a big note on the bathroom mirror to remind her about her new routine. Another trick she tried, once up, was resetting the alarm every ten minutes to remind her of the time.

The reason this technique worked well for Jill is that a group of activities were so closely linked in Jill's mind that it was only by rearranging them all that she was able to overcome the habit of being late. In doing so, she broke a complex chain of behavioral associations. Jill was also realistic about the strength of her habit, and used various techniques to reinforce her awareness and help her to act in a different way—for example, setting the alarm to go off every ten minutes as a time check. Although Jill did not choose to do this, she could have also looked at any underlying reasons behind her being late for work. In fact, Jill was having difficulties getting on with her new boss, and being late may have been a form of passive protest.

Instilling positive patterns

It is better to replace the old activity or behavior with something more positive rather than simply trying to stop the habit. For example, if you tend to go out drinking after work, it would be harder simply to stop and go home than to replace the habit with something healthier—such as going swimming or to a dance class—instead.

Many people have a mental "script" that runs repeatedly through their heads. Often, such scripts are negative, telling you that you are a failure, or comparing yourself unfavorably with anyone you meet. For example, you might lack confidence at social occasions, and have a script that says, "You're relentlessly dull. No one wants to talk to you. You're nothing." Giving yourself a positive script, which you consciously recite to yourself to displace the old, negative one, will feed your self-confidence; for example, a positive script might be: "I am an extremely warm, friendly person who likes people and has plenty to offer." Work on these positive reinforcements, and after a while they will become automatic.

Points for success

• Give yourself time to adjust to new behaviors.
• Reward yourself when you make progress—for example, treat yourself to a trip with friends to the cinema, or go for a swim after work.
• Ask a trusted friend to tell you when you are inadvertently slipping back into bad habits. You may want to make this a reciprocal arrangement for mutual support.
• Don't stop trying, even if you regress into your old behavior. Repeated efforts pay off.
• Affirm the changes you have made and try to describe your old habits in the past tense: "I used to be late for everything. Now I am well organized, respect other people's time, and am punctual for appointments."

DO I ALWAYS DO THAT?

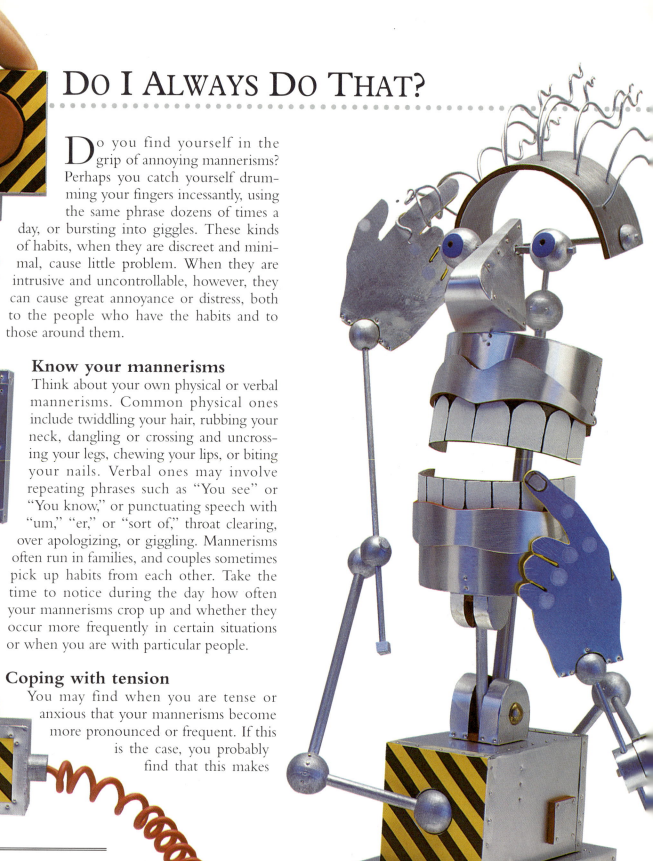

Do you find yourself in the grip of annoying mannerisms? Perhaps you catch yourself drumming your fingers incessantly, using the same phrase dozens of times a day, or bursting into giggles. These kinds of habits, when they are discreet and minimal, cause little problem. When they are intrusive and uncontrollable, however, they can cause great annoyance or distress, both to the people who have the habits and to those around them.

Know your mannerisms

Think about your own physical or verbal mannerisms. Common physical ones include twiddling your hair, rubbing your neck, dangling or crossing and uncrossing your legs, chewing your lips, or biting your nails. Verbal ones may involve repeating phrases such as "You see" or "You know," or punctuating speech with "um," "er," or "sort of," throat clearing, over apologizing, or giggling. Mannerisms often run in families, and couples sometimes pick up habits from each other. Take the time to notice during the day how often your mannerisms crop up and whether they occur more frequently in certain situations or when you are with particular people.

Coping with tension

You may find when you are tense or anxious that your mannerisms become more pronounced or frequent. If this is the case, you probably find that this makes

Remote control

If your mannerisms bother you, you may feel that you are like a machine, unable to control yourself.

you feel even more uncomfortable. Or perhaps you have a range of mannerisms that appear only when you are feeling nervous or stressed.

Mannerisms often start as a physical manifestation of anxiety and tension, the outward signs of inner disquiet. It's not for nothing, after all, that a moment heavy with suspense is commonly referred to as "nail-biting." Once they become established, mannerisms can become comforting in some way, so people resort to them habitually, even when they are not under stress.

Restricting your mannerisms

While it is not realistic to aim to eradicate all your mannerisms—indeed, not all mannerisms are unattractive or troublesome—you can work on restricting or eliminating those that particularly bother you. If you find that you are especially prone to nervous tics or verbal mannerisms in anxious or tense situations, you will probably feel more comfortable when you have your mannerisms under control. In these instances, try the following:

• When you are feeling anxious, try to get into the habit of practicing relaxation and visualization techniques (see below); these will help you to stay calm and restrict your nervous tics.

• Whether you are sitting or standing, keep your shoulders relaxed and loose. Let your arms hang by your side or your hands rest in your lap.

• When speaking, try to keep your voice at a measured pace by pausing between phrases; this gives you time to form your next sentence in your mind before you say it, and reduces the need to gain thinking time by repeating phrases such as "You see."

• If you tend to fidget, having a "toy" of some sort can help you control it. Small wooden or stone balls can be kept in your pocket and are very satisfying and calming to feel.

WHAT YOU CAN DO

If you find that your body gets the better of you when you are tense or anxious, the best and most effective way to get back in control is to learn to relax your body and your mind through relaxation and visualization techniques. Cutting down on nicotine, caffeine, and alcohol will also help to make you less twitchy. Taking a full-spectrum vitamin B supplement that works on the nervous system can also be beneficial.

Relaxation
Regularly practicing good breathing is very effective in aiding relaxation. Start by filling with air the lower half of your lungs, using the muscles of your rib cage and diaphragm. Place your hands against the bottom of your rib cage with your fingers lightly touching. If you are breathing in correctly, your fingers will draw apart. Hold your breath for a short while, then let the muscles relax as you breathe out. Concentrate on breathing slowly and evenly, inhaling and exhaling rhythmically and with no effort. A good position for these exercises is lying on your back with your knees half bent and supported by a cushion.

Visualization
Another useful technique is positive visualization. First picture yourself engaging in your mannerism—twiddling your hair, clasping and unclasping your hands, and so on— and acknowledge the discomfort you feel. Then conjure up an image of yourself that is relaxed, confident, and in control. Imagine yourself released from your particular mannerism—your hands dropping naturally to your sides, for example. Let yourself feel what it's like to be free from your habit. Notice how good you look, and how calm you feel. When you are in a situation where your mannerism normally appears, check yourself and bring to mind again your confident image. Repeat this visualization exercise at regular intervals to reinforce your positive self-image so that it becomes more natural.

ADDICTIVE BEHAVIOR

T HE LINE THAT DIVIDES habitual behavior and addictive behavior is a fine one. An addiction can sometimes begin as a habit, which then starts to take over your life. A useful way of separating them is to think of a habit as behavior that is within your control.

The problem with addictive behavior is that you don't control it, it controls you. Ironically, addictive behavior is often taken up in the first place as an unconscious attempt to control something, be it depression, anger, weight—even life and death. Eventually, the person loses control, and realizes they no longer have any choice over their behavior: it has become truly addictive.

A life of dependency
Admitting to yourself that you cannot function without your addiction is the first step to recovery.

IS IT ADDICTION?

The following are some of the ways to recognize addictive behavior:
• You feel you have no choice or control over it.
• You operate on "automatic"—i.e. the behavior is so entrenched that you are no longer aware of it.
• It feels necessary to repeat the behavior in order to gain more "kicks."

• It is something you do to avoid feelings of emptiness, blankness, depression, loneliness, anger, frustration, physical pain.
• Not to do it seems impossible—you simply couldn't cope without it.
• You spend a lot of emotional energy coping with it—feeling ashamed, guilty, not liking yourself.
• As a result, you spend a lot of time disguising and hiding the behavior from others.
• The behavior is entirely self-destructive, both physically and emotionally.
• The behavior interferes with your social life and your personal relationships.

What does it mean to you?
Addictions are intricately involved with our underlying emotions, which unconsciously cause the addictions and keep them going. For precisely this reason, it is often very difficult to overcome an addiction purely by behavioral means—something that can be used to alter habitual behavior. It isn't enough simply to become aware of what you're doing in order to try to stop doing it. You need to get to the root of what is causing the addiction. In order to identify the real cause of the problem, the addicted person may need outside help from a qualified therapist or counselor.

Very often, addictive behavior masks a deeper, psychological problem—it isn't so much the cigarette, the drink, or the food that is the difficulty, as its function. Compulsive working-out or running may in fact be a way of working off negative emotions or depression, running away from feelings that are painful; bingeing may well be a way of filling an emotional emptiness, and so on.

Addictive behavior is compulsive behavior—the person feels that without his or her addiction, whatever it may be, he or she will not be able to survive, or at the very least, cope. For example, anorexics often feel that if they do not keep tight control of their eating, they will let loose the greedy monster within themselves; the alcoholic similarly feels that without a drink, life would become increasingly overwhelming.

Admitting the problem

Addictive behavior is often a source of great shame and humiliation to the sufferer, who may spend a lot of time and emotional energy hiding his or her addiction from friends, family, and colleagues. As the addiction worsens or grows stronger, however, it is increasingly difficult to hide it from the world.

To many people, it is shameful and humiliating to admit to needing something to the extent that it runs your life. Often the people around the addict will collude in order not to cause him or her, or themselves, pain and embarrassment. Of course, this makes it even more difficult for the sufferer to change. Sometimes this situation may go on for years, until someone is able to speak the truth, at a time when the addict is able to hear it.

One of the greatest problems with addictive behavior is admitting to it—even to yourself. Yet this is the first step toward changing it, and taking control of your situation. Addicts need to be made aware that many, many people have already been in a comparable situation, and that there really need be no stigma involved in addiction. Help and support are essential for the addict, who needs to know that there is the solid backing of a person nearby that he or she can call. This is why so many self-help groups have a system whereby a person is allocated a supporter, or "buddy," whom they can contact when they feel particularly alone, or tempted to give in to their addiction.

SHOPPING ADDICTS

Daniel "had it all," as his friends said: he was good-looking, bright, had a good job, and a loving girlfriend. Daniel also had very expensive tastes, and nothing was ever good enough for him or his friends. The fact that he spent money as fast as he earned it wasn't even noticed by anyone else. But no one knew that Daniel felt compelled to buy something expensive daily. If he didn't, he became very depressed.

Although his large salary had offset his spending for a while, it soon came to the attention of his bank that Daniel was very overdrawn and in debt to the tune of several thousand dollars. When he was asked to come in to see the bank manager—a young man Daniel's age—he was mortified. How was he going to explain this to his friends and family?

Getting help

Shopping and spending addictions share with all addictions the sufferer's need for an object that will magically, instantly make them feel better. In Daniel's case, it was necessary to give himself an expensive present every day in order to keep alive his fragile sense of self-worth. Because this feeling only lasted a very short time, it was necessary for him to constantly "feed" this need. When his addiction was made public, and he was forced to confront how serious it was, in the company of someone who was his equal in every other way, Daniel felt terrible shame.

Although he thought that he would never be the sort of person who needed to see a "shrink," in desperation Daniel sought out a counselor. He was helped to face his feelings of inadequacy and see how shopping had stopped him from addressing the real issues—that he felt needy and unlovable.

ADDICTED TO WORK

Western society has condoned and encouraged work as a source of pride, satisfaction, and self-esteem for the last few hundred years. For many people, it does fulfill this function, but the fact that for some people work can easily become an addiction shows that even something that starts out by being healthy and useful can become self-destructive.

Compete and fail

Competition can play a major role in an addiction to work, as it did for Alan. From the moment he arrived at his desk until he went home, he never seemed to stop. He arrived at work earlier than the others, and left after everyone else—he even began to come into the office on weekends. While Alan won the praise and acknowledgment of his boss

(who may also have been a workaholic), his girl-friend felt otherwise: Alan was always late coming home, he forgot dates they had arranged together; and he talked non-stop about work. When his girl-friend gave Alan an ultimatum to decide between her and his job, he had to choose work.

The need to please the boss, to be special and better than others, has its roots in childhood, when perhaps a person felt overlooked, or that they weren't as good as his or her brothers and sisters. The feeling of being needed or indispensable is a strong one, and people such as Alan often feel their workplace will collapse without them. When they discover that they aren't essential, or when their bodies say "no more," they can feel overwhelmed by worthlessness, or that their entire life is over.

AVOIDING FEELINGS

It is common for people to run away from other areas of their life by burying themselves in their job. Some people use work as a way of avoiding intimacy, of running away from demands made on them by their partners, or of backing away from finding a partner in the first place. For others, work is the only thing they have: outside their job they may be totally isolated. It is often those who live such lonely lives who turn to their jobs for comfort.

What lies behind an addiction to work may be an avoidance of loneliness, depression, and emptiness, disguised by constant activity. An addiction to work is often overlooked; what people believe they are seeing isn't an addict, but someone who is "keen," "enthusiastic," or "ambitious"—all qualities our society actively encourages. In addition, in today's economic climate, competition in many fields is intense. Yet, like other addictions, it is behavior that disguises a person's real needs.

Doctors are swamped by patients showing the physical manifestations of overwork: backache, headache, chronic fatigue syndrome, chronic illness of any kind, stomach problems, sexual difficulties, and a variety of emotional and psychological symptoms. Addiction to work is similar to many other addictions: it is a learned behavior that is repeated compulsively to satisfy a person's emotional needs or fears.

All work and no play
The workaholic can no longer choose whether to work or play: he or she is compelled to stay on the job. But not taking leisure time doesn't make you more effective at work—quite the opposite. Research has shown that workaholics make more mistakes, and cost companies more money as a result, than their better-adjusted colleagues.

ARE YOU A WORKAHOLIC?

It's often difficult to pinpoint the difference between working for enjoyment and working because you feel compelled to do so. In a similar way to considering the difference between habits and addictions, there can be a gray area where the good feelings you may receive from working hard gradually become something that take over your life, leaving no space for anything else.

People are far better at disguising the truth from themselves than from others. Because the people around you frequently see what is happening to you before you do, it's useful to ask your partner, a close friend, or colleagues what they think about your work habits. Their responses may not be what you expected.

Avoiding workaholism

You may be surprised by the amount of time you spend at work, either in the workplace or at home. If it is much more than an average of 35 to 40 hours per week, you should ask yourself why you are allowing your job to dominate your life.

Often the cause of a need to overwork, like other addictions, lies in some other area of the person's life. The addiction is taking the place of something that has either been lost, or is not there—a close relationship or a sense of worth, for example. It can also be a means of distracting yourself from painful feelings or of giving yourself a sense of purpose that might otherwise be lacking in your life.

As with all addictions, the first step is to acknowledge you have a problem. Once you have done this, you will be on the way to finding out why you have this problem. This may firstly involve facing up to whatever it is that you are avoiding by working so hard, and then by exploring the feelings that surround it.

Sometimes people who have previously worked in a healthy way find that workaholism is creeping up on them. If you are aware of the signs of impending workaholism, you may be able to catch it before it takes over your life. Another common situation is that you start a new job only to find that the culture within that workplace promotes workaholism. In this case, it may be necessary to set the ground rules at the beginning, working out how many hours you are prepared to give.

It is not easy to recognize or to admit to work addiction in a society that is permeated with messages that positively reinforce the idea of the work ethic, and it can be especially hard if you are employed by an organization that actively encourages workaholism. In such organizations, working long hours is seen as a sign of commitment to the company, and in some cases the job could not possibly be done in the time officially allocated to it.

HOW HARD DO YOU WORK?

The following questions will give you some idea of whether you are a workaholic. Ask yourself how far you come outside the norm in relation to work:

• Are you one of the first to arrive? And the last to leave? How often does this happen?
• How many hours are you expected to work? How many hours do you actually work?
• When sick, do you take time off work in order to recover, or do you carry on regardless?

Get the balance right
Many workaholics believe they are superproductive, but they overvalue the necessity of their work.

Unhappily, such organizations are all too common. To many in these working environments, workaholism is an acceptable addiction and as such is not treated with the seriousness it deserves. But the reality is that workaholism ruins lives. Relationships can break down, children may feel their parent has abandoned them, and the workaholic's health will eventually suffer.

Many people have recovered from workaholism, and report that their lives are richer and more satisfying as a result. Here are some of the steps that have proved useful to workaholics in recovery:

• Remove yourself from the workplace for a period of leave. Taking a break gives you the necessary distance to re-examine your priorities and reach a new and healthier perspective on your life.
• Enlist the support of a friend or a counselor. This will ensure that when you return to work you have strategies in place for coping with your addiction.
• Re-examine your working life. Some workaholics opt for a new job or career that does not make the same intolerable demands on their time and is more rewarding personally. But you need to stay alert to the triggers that set off your addiction.

• Are your workmates your only friends?
• Do you tend to work on the weekend? How much and how often? And what effect would it have on your job if you didn't do this extra work?
• Do you take the vacations to which you are entitled?
• Do the people close to you seem affected by your work? In what way?
• Have you ever cancelled social events due to work?
• Do you generally take work with you when you have to be away from the office, for instance on vacation?

• When did you last do something enjoyable after work, or on the weekend? Did you do this alone, or with someone else?
• Do you define yourself by what you do as a job?
• What would you do if you lost your job?
• Do you find it difficult to stop "doing," even outside work, and relax?

EATING HABITS

Are you happy with what you eat? Do you basically eat a healthy, balanced diet, choosing the foods that are good for you, while feeling able to have French fries or chocolate occasionally without agonizing over it? Or do you swing wildly between gorging on junk food, then berating yourself for "being bad" and half-starving yourself on a crash diet of cottage cheese and crispbread? For many of us, even if we are well versed in nutrition, it is surprisingly difficult consistently to eat what's best for us.

One of the problems of maintaining a balanced approach to food is that eating is a very basic, primitive human activity, and has many associations with maternal care—and thus with love, nurturing, and comfort. As adults, we may turn to food to fill feelings of loneliness, emptiness, or distress. Children are often given a sweet if they have hurt themselves, to stop them crying, or to cheer them up, which can form a link between sweets and comfort. Do you find you tend to "treat" yourself with something sweet when you have had a particularly rough day or are feeling down? Many people have regular cravings for sweet, starchy foods, such as chocolate, cakes, and potato chips, which they may equate with holidays, special treats, or even with "forbidden" pleasure—foods are often linked to childhood memories.

The dieting trap

Understanding that we are often trying to meet our emotional needs when we crave "comfort" foods may help us to find a more balanced approach to eating—and dieting. By learning to recognize the difference between real hunger and emotional hunger—and feeding them in appropriate ways—we will be less caught in the trap of eating too much "bad" food and then dieting, torn between guilt and temptation.

For many people, dieting has become both a source of hope and a prison: losing weight will solve all their problems—of belonging, self-esteem, attractiveness, health. At the same time they are trapped—by their genetic make-up, which dictates their basic body shape and size, and by an unattainable vision of perfection. Many people are unaware of the emotional currency that lies behind their dieting habits. The questions on the next page may help you to identify what some of this might be.

If you have difficulties about food and dieting, the guidelines in the box opposite may help you return to a healthier path. The next time you have a food craving, stop and try to get in touch with what you are feeling—it might open some doors on to what is really going on inside you.

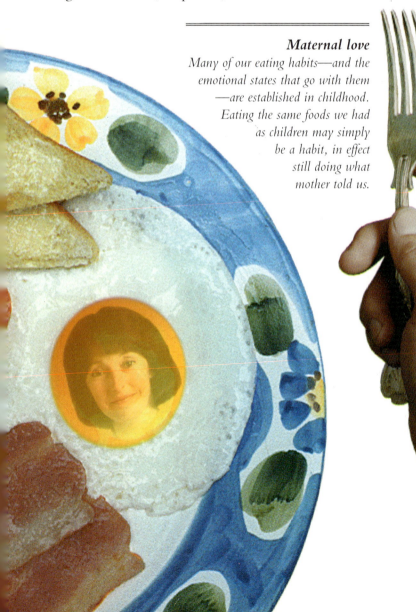

Maternal love
Many of our eating habits—and the emotional states that go with them —are established in childhood. Eating the same foods we had as children may simply be a habit, in effect still doing what mother told us.

Comfort food?
Childhood treats often turn into comfort food in times of stress.

Keeping track

Our relationship to food is a powerful indicator of our inner selves—how we feel about ourselves and how we relate to others. What do your answers to the following questions say about you?:
• Do you like to cook? For yourself or only for others? Is food something that you don't "allow" yourself to enjoy?
• Do you prefer to eat in company or alone? If eating is a sociable activity for you, it is likely that you are happy to be around other people. If eating is fraught with guilt and a fear of gaining weight, you may be afraid of losing control and showing your need—not just for food, but for love and attention.
• Do you eat while doing something else—watching TV, reading the newspaper, talking?
• What are your favorite foods? Off the top of your head, what memories do they hold for you?
• Do you tend to eat quickly? If so, food and eating may have ceased to give you pleasure.

Eating disorders

For people with severe eating disorders such as compulsive eating, bulimia, and anorexia nervosa, eating is a painful battleground that expresses very deep emotional distress, the reasons for which are well hidden from the sufferer and those who try to help him or her. Each case has its unique profile, but some common threads have emerged. With such extreme conditions, extreme emotions are present: deep shame; sorrow, often over failed relationships; rage and anger directed at the self; a need to feel in control in a life where little real control is felt. In such cases, trying to alter food habits is rarely effective. The underlying causes need to be brought out into the open and resolved, usually with the help of a professional.

BACK TO HEALTH

It's important to be realistic about the complexity of your eating habits—they have probably been ingrained in you during years of repetitive behavior. The guidelines here will help you to set out well-formed goals that are achievable for *you*.

To start with, break your end target into small, easy steps—don't try to do everything at once, as this can set you up for disappointment.

Group healing

Many eating difficulties are relieved by being part of a group, as sharing a problem can be a great relief and comfort. People with eating problems tend to feel ashamed of themselves and respond well to being with others who understand.

Understand yourself

A common phenomenon when trying to change is to find yourself splitting into the you who wants to change, and the you who wants to stay the same. The former you may sound a bit like a scolding parent: "Now, come on, you can't have any more." The other voice is often the child: "But I want more." Try to develop a way of talking to yourself that is both understanding and firm: "I really love it, but I've had enough now."

Change the circumstances

Try making subtle changes in the way you behave around food. For one week write down all you can about your eating habits, paying special attention to what, when, how you eat, and your mood. This will give you an insight into your eating pattern, which you can then change.

Many people with eating problems tend to eat alone. Try to eat in public, or invite a friend to a meal regularly. If you tend to eat junk foods, try to change to healthier ones, a little at a time. If you eat when depressed, go to a movie, or do something you enjoy that doesn't involve food.

ADDICTED TO EXERCISE

Following an exercise plan is such a socially acceptable activity that it is not always easy to spot when a desire to exercise has turned into an addiction. What separates an exercise addict from the average keep-fitter is that he or she is no longer able to choose whether or not to work out, but is *compelled* to exercise. Without a regular exercise "fix," the addict suffers from a range of psychological withdrawal symptoms that include irritability, panic, tension, and even guilt.

A case of control

A desire for control is often at the root of an addiction. To be able to mold their bodies to an ideal shape, size, and weight gives some people a feeling of power that is otherwise lacking in their lives. Underneath they feel a failure, which they compensate for by running farther and farther, swimming faster and faster, and so on. In this way the behavior becomes a vital source of self-esteem.

For people with eating disorders, working out is often a means of assuaging guilt for overeating—for their unforgivable lapses of control. They feel that they must work off any weight that they might possibly have gained, and so a vicious circle of bingeing and working out may be put into motion. Going to the gym becomes a metaphor for regaining control.

Exercising to forget

Constant exercise may also be a way of avoiding other painful feelings or situations—such as a fear of intimacy with people or a difficult home life. Wendy, for example, had always been slightly

An uncomfortable fit?
Over-exercising is often part of forcing your body to fit an over-idealized image that springs from poor self-esteem.

overweight as a child. When she reached young adulthood, she suffered from feelings of shame and self-consciousness about her body, feeling that she was too fat. Wendy put herself on a strict diet, and began to work out relentlessly at her local gym. After a few months, having lost both weight and inches, she felt really good: in control and strong. For the first time in her life, Wendy believed she looked attractive. She noticed, however, that if she couldn't make it to the gym for any reason, she became anxious that she would start getting fat again. She knew that this wasn't logical; it was as if the gym gave her a sense of power and control without which she would lose her only source of self-esteem. Far from being in control of her life, Wendy had become addicted to exercise.

Competing with yourself

Are you someone who enjoys the competitive element of exercise? Whether competing with others or with yourself, you might find that you are constantly pushing yourself, trying to reach an impossible target. This type of competitiveness can become addictive because nothing is ever good enough: The exercise addict never feels satisfied and constantly strives to do better. And if you should fall behind, you may feel intense guilt, berating and sometimes punishing yourself by following an even stricter exercise regime.

Running free

Once a dependency has been recognized, it *is* possible to break free. If the addiction has arisen as a result of denying difficult personal issues, then addressing these—perhaps with the help of a counselor, therapist, or self-help group—will help you to put your life into perspective, including the addiction to exercise. Familiarizing yourself with some of the exercise myths, which are addressed in detail in *Body Traps* by Dr. Judith Rodin, may also help you to draw up a sensible exercise program.

One major myth is that the more you exercise, the healthier you will become. There is such a thing as over-exercising, and the physical benefits to be gained by pushing yourself to ever-greater limits are minimal, if any—in fact, you could very easily injure yourself. A moderate exercise program is perfectly adequate for your health needs. If it no longer seems enough for you, then it might be time to seek help.

TAKING IT TOO FAR?

How can you tell if you are addicted to exercise? Read the following questions, answering each one Yes or No.
• Do you exercise nearly every day, and in all kinds of weather?
• Has the amount of time you spend exercising increased in the last six months?
• Do you exercise no matter how you are feeling?
• If you have had a minor injury, have you still exercised, even if this went against doctor's orders?
• Would you cancel social engagements rather than miss an exercise class or gym session?
• Do you feel tense and irritable if you aren't able to exercise?
• Have you lost any real enjoyment for exercise; has it become a grueling ritual?
If you answered yes to more than four questions, then exercise may have become an addictive substitute for something else, and you may have to look at why you need to do it.

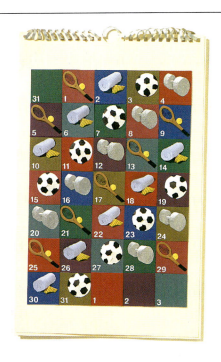

GET OFF THE HOOK

WHEN WE ARE BEING HONEST with ourselves, most of us know what our addictions are and how great a hold they have on our lives. However, because we find it difficult to change our behavior, we look for reasons to justify it. One very common excuse is the "I'm addicted, I can't help it, I guess I'm stuck with it now" approach. Or we may choose to ignore the potentially harmful effects of our particular vices, and claim to be in charge of the situation: "I'm not addicted to cigarettes, I just enjoy smoking. I could give up any time I wanted to;" "I don't have a problem with alcohol—I just know how to relax and have a good time;" "Why should I give up coffee? Life would be so dull without some vices."

All of these justifications for addictions are ways of abdicating our personal responsibility for taking care of ourselves and taking control of our lives. Owning your behavior as something you *choose* to do makes it easier to overcome it using your ability to think, reason, and decide.

Physical or psychological?

With some addictions, particularly to cigarettes, people feel that they won't be able to give up because of the physical discomfort that withdrawal will bring. In fact, the physical addiction is usually minor, but the psychological dependence often produces physical feelings of craving and, if not satisfied, discomfort.

When a smoker lights up and takes his first puff of the day, he gets a kind of fix from the sudden rush of nicotine, and his heartbeat speeds up. Studies reveal, however, that smokers who have been given nicotine that is released more slowly into their bodies still experience a strong urge to smoke. This suggests that a simple addiction to nicotine is not the only reason for smoking. The craving for a cigarette may indeed be felt strongly as a physical need, but the psychological need is also a significant factor.

Addictive behaviors are often conditioned reflexes, triggered by a learned association formed between the behavior and certain feelings, such as anxiety, or feeling awkward or unloved. Many people feel that other triggers set them off—for example, they may automatically light a cigarette when they sit down to relax with

How hooked are you?
To break free, the addict must face the self-justification and denial involved in his or her addiction.

a cup of coffee, or they may always have several alcoholic drinks when at a party or out with friends "just to be sociable" or because "everyone does it, don't they?" Often, these surface reasons mask deeper feelings, perhaps of low self-esteem or a feeling of isolation and wanting to belong and be accepted.

The addictive personality

Some people seem to be more prone than others to addictions. Perhaps you know someone who used to smoke or drink heavily, then suddenly turned over a new leaf and now exercises fanatically, going to the gym every day, or becoming obsessed by a new sport or interest. The person may even describe him- or herself jokingly as having "an addictive personality." Do you find that you quickly move to extremes of behavior in this way? Many people with addictions suffer from feelings of inadequacy, believing that they are inferior to others.

Having a familiar "support" to turn to when you're feeling down or stressed can be very comforting. However, using addictions as a prop because of a fear of experiencing unpleasant or uncomfortable feelings merely reduces your tolerance of frustration and emotional pain, rather than strengthening your capacity to work through problems. The instant gratification feels good at the time, but is often followed by a further drop in mood as the person feels a degree of self-loathing at having given in to the addiction.

Freeing yourself

Often, the first step in reducing the hold that an addiction has on you is to take back the responsibility for having it, and say to yourself, "I have a problem, but I now choose to make the changes and do the work necessary to free myself from it." Another decisive factor in overcoming an addiction is that you must really want to do it for yourself; if you are merely responding to pressure or nagging from someone else, your resolve is likely to waver and you may also start to resent the other person. Think about what you need to help you give up—would you benefit from tackling the addiction with the help of a support group or a friend who wants to combat an addiction, too? If the addiction is partly triggered by feelings of isolation, having the support of others can be especially helpful.

RAISE YOUR AWARENESS

This exercise helps you become more aware of why you have an addiction. Every time you feel the urge to carry out an addictive or habitual behavior, stop for a moment and think about how you feel, then complete the statements below to form a record in a notebook, and include the date and time. Over a period of even just a few days you should be able to see a pattern emerging of the thoughts and feelings that trigger your addictive behavior, and how these are reinforced repeatedly.
• Right now, I am feeling… (e.g. tense, bored, lonely, anxious, angry, inadequate, hungry, depressed)
• I feel like this because… (e.g. I've just argued with my partner, I'm all alone, I can't cope)
• If I were to do this behavior, I would feel… (e.g. fulfilled, relieved, full, relaxed)
• If I don't do this behavior, I will feel… (e.g. out of control, terrible)

Fight the impulse

Your answers to the above will help you start to become aware of exactly what thoughts and feelings you experience in the moments before you act. Try to hold off the impulse for a few minutes, while you take the time to ask yourself the questions. You may find that by delaying instant gratification in this way, the intense urge to carry out the addictive or habitual behavior starts to fade.

It may well be very difficult at first, and many people find it helpful to turn to others for support while they are battling against their addiction. Having a temporary displacement activity to take the place of the addiction can be useful. For example, you could decide to brush your teeth every time you feel a very strong craving for chocolate, then run your tongue over your teeth, relishing the fresh, minty taste, and clean feeling. Or you can choose to do something similar but harmless, such as having a herb tea when you want a cup of coffee.

GIVING UP SMOKING

Every smoker is individual. Everyone has different characteristics and smokes for their own reasons. You may be an introvert, not needing much stimulation from the outside world, and smoke to calm yourself down; or perhaps you are an extrovert, seeking constant arousal, and using smoking as a way to stimulate your brain and your body. Scientists have shown that people smoke both to be stimulated and to calm down. Which applies to you? Do you smoke because you enjoy the physical stimulation, in order to feel confident in stressful situations, or because you feel more effective and creative after a nicotine surge, for example?

Personal campaign

Since smoking is an individual matter, it's essential that your stop-smoking campaign is tailor-made for you. Only you can decide what makes you smoke, and only you can create a plan of action to kick your habit.

Moving on
You have the freedom to break away from your habit.

Different kinds of smoking

Although everyone's smoking habit is different, all reasons for smoking can be grouped into the following categories. Which reasons apply to you?

Indulgent
- I smoke when I'm comfortable and relaxed.
- I enjoy smoking after a meal or after sex.
- I smoke only when I'm not in a hurry.

Social
- I feel relaxed with people when I'm smoking.
- I feel more confident and in control with others.
- I tend to smoke more at social occasions.

Physical
- I smoke to have something in my mouth.
- I find handling a cigarette pleasurable.
- I enjoy watching the smoke as I exhale.

Stimulation
- I smoke when I'm in a hurry or busy.
- I smoke when I'm tired, in order to wake up.
- Smoking helps me to think or to concentrate.
- Smoking cheers me up.

Addictive
- I can't bear ever to run out of cigarettes.
- I begin to crave a cigarette after a certain time.

Automatic
- I'm not always aware that I'm smoking.
- I sometimes light a cigarette before one is out.
- I sometimes don't remember lighting a cigarette.

Breaking the habit

If you smoke occasionally, and only to relax and in social situations, you are probably not that addicted to cigarettes. This means that, while you still have to reassess your life, you may find it easier to give up smoking than if you smoke out of a need for stimulation, or because you are addicted or doing it automatically.

Most addicted smokers consider giving up only when a physical symptom caused by smoking appears. You will need very persuasive reasons for not smoking, and will have to remind yourself of these constantly to fight off both your psychological dependency and a strong need for nicotine. You may find it helpful to monitor the number of cigarettes you smoke and then work out a daily allowance, gradually cutting down the number. For further advice on giving up, see the box, right.

TIPS TO QUIT

Every smoker finds their own route to becoming an ex-smoker. Particular therapies and practical tips work for some people and not others. The trick is to find what helps you. For some, becoming an ex-smoker is a gradual process of changing their smoking pattern; for others it is a case of making a decision and sticking to it. Try whichever of the following tips you feel comfortable with:
- Work out how much money you will save, and how to spend it.
- Make a list of all the reasons why you want to stop smoking. Read your list whenever you feel the urge to smoke.

Bright future
Look ahead to being an ex-smoker and reward yourself on the way— perhaps with a holiday.

- Make sure that you are stopping for *yourself*.
- Try to avoid other smokers, or going places where people are likely to smoke.
- Give up now, and rely on willpower to see you through. Don't be tempted to have even one smoke.
- Create no-smoking areas in your own home, making them as cosy as possible.
- Try to reduce your desire to smoke. For example, limit your smoking to outside, regardless of the weather conditions; or smoke rapidly so that it makes you feel ill.
- Give yourself set times to stop smoking; for example, go without your lunchtime cigarette.
- Wean yourself off nicotine, perhaps with the help of nicotine replacement patches, which have fewer toxins than cigarettes.
- Learn to relax, as tension can bring on reactions that feel like withdrawal symptoms.
- Don't force yourself to commit to doing without nicotine for ever.
- Try alternative therapies such as acupuncture and hypnotherapy, which can help beat cravings.
- Go on a stop smoking course—the support of a group and the follow-up usually provided have proved a successful route for many ex-smokers.

CUTTING DOWN ON ALCOHOL

Like smoking, drinking can become a physiological addiction. However, while smoking is straightforwardly destructive to health, deciding whether you should drink alcohol, and how much, involves considering the social and psychological place of alcohol in your life.

How much is too much?

For many people, drinking alcohol is an integral part of their social life, and presents no problem. However, some feel confused about how much alcohol is healthy. This confusion is compounded because there are reports that drinking some alcohol has positive benefits. Countries such as Britain and Australia have advisory limits on alcohol consumption. These are 21 units per week for men and 14 units for women, a unit being a glass of wine or beer, or a small measure of spirits. If you drink much more, consider cutting down on your consumption and look at whether you are addicted. Addictive behaviors tend to reinforce each other, and you may find that if you smoke while you drink, both problems have to be tackled together.

Like any other addiction, if you feel you are drinking too much it is a good idea to look at why you drink, and address any problems you are avoiding. Perhaps alcohol relaxes you and makes you feel more confident socially, or maybe you are trying to escape from feelings of frustration, tension, or unhappiness. However, drinking can also cause such problems, and it can be difficult to work out which came first. Facing up to these feelings, perhaps with the help of a counselor, will help you gain control of your drinking.

Controlled drinking

Many people who are concerned about their drinking will be able to find a way to cut it down, rather than having to abstain altogether. Keeping a drink diary can help you work out when you are drinking. Write down at which times in the day and week you drink, how you feel at the time, and how you react afterwards. This will enable you to see what makes you drink in particular circumstances. When you are drinking alcohol, drink it with

Increasing isolation
Although people often drink to make themselves more socially confident, an over-dependence on alcohol can end up having the opposite effect.

awareness and enjoyment, rather than just drinking unconsciously. It may help to pour your drink into a smaller glass, and then sip it slowly to make it last longer. Also, set aside one or two days in the week when you drink low-alcohol wine or lager, or non-alcoholic beverages.

When to stop

If, when you drink, you often become very drunk, lose consciousness, or don't remember anything the next day, then you will need medical advice and assistance to stop drinking. Your self-esteem will improve enormously once you have taken the brave step of exerting control over your drinking.

Total abstinence is the goal for people who have serious problems with alcohol. This method is used by self-help support groups, such as Alcoholics Anonymous, who believe that once an alcoholic, always an alcoholic, and that drinking any alcohol

at all can tip a person back into their previous patterns of abuse. In order to break this chain, Al-Anon hold regular meetings where people can gain support in overcoming their alcoholism.

For very serious, long-term drinking problems, it may be necessary to go to a detoxification clinic. This treatment often includes aversion therapy, which involves consuming a drug that causes the drinker to feel nauseated if he or she drinks alcohol. Psychotherapy, counseling, and group work are used in conjunction with this treatment. If your drinking is out of control to this extent, it is essential that you get help now.

Alternatively, you may be suffering because a family member is abusing alcohol. In this case, there may not be anything you can do to stop him or her, but you can get help for yourself. Attending a self-help group for relatives of alcoholics, such as Al-Anon, can offer a valuable means of support.

THE LOVE ADDICTION CYCLE

THERE IS A TYPE of addiction that is less recognized than a dependency on alcohol or drugs, but which has great potential to hurt individuals and ruin relationships—love addiction. Some people become addicted to the early, exciting phases of a new relationship and keep trying to re-create this idyll, while others are locked into unsatisfactory relationships with people who do not return their love. Like addicts to chemical substances, love addicts often do not recognize the patterns they are playing out time and again. In order to break their cycle of addiction, they need to re-examine their values and motivations.

Romance addicts

Many people are in love with love—addicted to the thrilling, heady pleasure of falling in love. For a while the new relationship seems perfect. However, as the relationship develops, this intense passion inevitably begins to fade.

__Same old tune__
Love addicts play out the same patterns time and again with successive partners, becoming depressed as they are unable to foster a happy relationship.

Some addicts interpret this as a sign that the relationship is over, while others redouble their efforts to re-create high romance even if the partner is trying to withdraw. Love addicts may blame their partner for not coming up to scratch and may line up another partner, who, they feel, will live up to their expectations. However, the pattern repeats itself with the new partner.

An addiction to the seemingly perfect love affair often masks a love addict's deep-seated sense of inadequacy. He or she looks to a "perfect" person to make his or her life more worthwhile.

Destructive relationships

Other love addicts find themselves locked into a destructive relationship with one partner. In many cases, owing to their emotional needs not being met when they were children, they choose emotionally "distant" people with problems on whom they can pour all their love. This is especially common in love-addicted women, who become caregivers in order to fill their own unmet need for affection.

Addicts of this kind are not attracted to stable men who will love them as they deserve. They believe that, simply because of who they are, they don't deserve love, and try to earn it by doing anything for their partner. Yet underneath their helpfulness they are really controlling their partner, trying to change him. Addicts have a high tolerance for emotional pain and do not see that the relationship is harmful.

Curing love addiction

Being a love addict makes it impossible to develop a healthy, loving relationship. Love addicts are trapped in a cycle of undervaluing themselves and looking to other people—or to "love"—to make them feel good about themselves. Therapy seeks to halt and correct the addict's perceptions.

The first stage in curing love addiction is to realize what is happening and to want to change it. Then the addict needs to get help—usually from a trained therapist or counselor, who will help the addict face his or her own problems and shortcomings. As the addict begins to take control of his or her own life, self-appreciation grows and the person becomes able to make new, healthy choices about love relationships.

HEALTHY RELATIONSHIPS

Many love addicts have never had a healthy relationship and so don't recognize when a relationship is either contributing to their well-being or harming them. One of the most important elements in fostering a healthy relationship is to have a realistic view of both the relationship and your partner. You can't expect either to be perfect, or transform your life. Both have a mixture of positive and negative aspects—ranging from joy, through comfort, to discomfort, and even pain. Much of a relationship is spent in the companionable performance of routine tasks—not in wild, passionate moments.

You also need to have a realistic view of yourself, to accept your strengths and your shortcomings, and to take responsibility for your personal growth rather than expecting your partner to be your savior. In a healthy relationship you take care of your own emotional needs. You can also support your partner without trying to control him or her.

Do not expect that you and your partner will always agree. Learning to compromise as well as communicate clearly and kindly helps you to enjoy your partner despite the differences between you.

ARE YOU STUCK ON LOVE?

Are you a love addict? Do you get "high" on heady feelings of romantic love and seek to re-create them over and over? Or do you instigate relationships with great intensity, but then back out hastily when you feel threatened by intimacy?

Love addiction is all a question of degree. If you have on only one or two occasions felt some of the typical addicted symptoms already described on pages 92–93, you are probably not addicted. If, however, you find yourself living out the same relationship pattern repeatedly, you may have a problem. To assess your own pattern of love behavior, answer the questions in the following quiz. Give yourself no points each time you answered "never"; one point for "with one partner"; two points for "with a few partners"; and three points every time you answered "with every partner." Then carefully read through the questions again, marking which ones you think particularly apply to your present or most recent partner. An analysis of your score appears on page 139.

Have you ever...

1. felt that you are incredibly lucky to be with such a perfect partner?
2. fallen in love when you were feeling vulnerable or not good about yourself?
3. done or said anything to a potential partner to make them want you?
4. gained a sense of triumph from your conquest?
5. been attracted to a person who has a sense of urgent passion?
6. been attracted to an emotionally troubled person?
7. been more aware of the needs of your partner than of your own?
8. relied on your partner to supply your own feelings of self-worth?

Fast drive
For some people, sex and relationships are a matter of performance rather than love. Does this describe you?

9. believed that, if your partner solved their problems, yours would be solved too?

10. felt that your partner really needs you?

11. thought about your relationship all the time?

12. got high on your partner's adulation?

13. intensively sought activities outside the relationship to keep you away from your partner?

14. waited by the phone for your partner to call?

15. checked up on your partner or followed them?

16. been treated badly by your partner?

17. excused your lover's bad temper and ill treatment of you?

18. loved your partner more if he or she was also attached to another and therefore unavailable?

19. been loving and helpful so that your partner will change and start being pleasant?

20. tried to control your partner as a way to tolerate his or her abusive behavior?

21. felt engulfed and controlled by your partner?

22. needed to be right and in control all the time?

23. felt that sex is about performance?

24. become bored when the passion fades?

25. thought that your partner didn't live up to your expectations?

26. consistently blamed your partner for not coming up to scratch?

27. had a one-night stand?

28. cheated on a partner?

29. found it difficult to end a relationship even when you know it is not working?

30. withdrawn suddenly from your partner after a period of great intensity?

31. been the one to end a relationship?

32. felt the need to get even with an ex-partner?

33. believed that your next relationship will work?

34. got straight into another affair after a break-up?

Being ignored?

Some men may ignore their girlfriends when they are out together. If this happens to you, do you mind?

SEX ADDICTION

I s it possible for someone to become addicted to sex? Psychologists are increasingly willing to accept that some people do become sexually addicted—by this they mean a person feels powerless to change his or her pattern of behavior, and suffers severe physiological and psychological symptoms if the desire for sex is frustrated or denied. Any type of behavior may be described as addictive if it becomes self-destructive, unmanageable, inflexible, beyond conscious control, and liable to escalate in frequency and risk. Sex addiction is all these things.

Sexual addiction involves a craving for sex that is so overwhelming that the person restructures his or her life around seeking opportunities for sexual gratification. What often drives people to compulsive sexual behavior is a fundamental lack of self-worth—it is

Off the shelf
Some people have an urgent need to pick a sexual partner with no more care than they would select a can of beans.

as if the addict is able to feel needed, alive, and vital only through sex. Such feelings of low self-esteem may stem from a childhood in which affection was not shown, or parental approval was lacking. Sometimes, children who have been sexually abused resort to sexually addictive behavior as adults: For them, sex may then become a means of getting love or affection, not expressing it, and they may need the help of a qualified counselor or therapist.

Highs and lows

People who describe themselves as sex addicts commonly report that they feel a "high" of improved self-esteem during sexual encounters; this elation is, however, quickly followed by depression, restlessness, and craving—feelings that drive them to repeat sexual contact, and so re-affirm their sense of self-worth.

People addicted to sex are likely to have sexual encounters that focus less on intimacy than on the feelings of release achieved through orgasm. They frequently disregard the needs of their partners, or manipulate them into fulfilling their own needs by emotional blackmail or coercion. They may experience guilt or even disgust about their behavior, but are overwhelmed by the need to persist. At its

worst, compulsive sexual behavior may be danger-ous or even life-threatening, as the addict ceases to exercise sufficient care in choosing his or her part-ners, and risks exposure to sexually transmitted dis-eases, violence, or abuse.

If you would describe yourself as addicted to sex, you may need the help of a qualified therapist or counselor, but the following points may help you to restore a sense of perspective:

1. Get to know your own body. Sex addicts often expect others to stimulate them, and do not under-stand their own arousal pattern, or realize that they may resort to bullying their partners.

2. Don't rush sex. Give yourself and your partner plenty of time to explore your bodies and, most importantly, your feelings. Do you feel scared? Are you tense and anxious? Talk to your partner about these feelings.

3. If your partner appears to be addicted to sex, don't collude in his or her behavior. Make sure you know your own sexual needs, and ask for them to be considered and respected. Do not allow yourself to be forced to take part in a sexual activity you dislike simply to please your partner.

SEX AND LOVE

In today's relatively relaxed moral climate, in which our culture places such enormous emphasis on all aspects of sexual desirability—especially as a criterion of self-fulfillment—it may be difficult to remember that your sexual relationships alone, although undoubtedly a very important part of your life, do not exclusively define your self-worth. While sex can be used as a way of expressing or disguising your deepest feelings, it is important to bear in mind what sex is not.

What sex isn't

The American psychologist Charlotte Davis Kasl, in her book *Women, Sex & Addiction*, makes the following points:

• Sex is not proof of being loved
• Sex is not proof of loving someone
• Sex is not proof of being attractive
• Sex doesn't make anyone important
• Sex doesn't cure problems
• Sex is not nurture
• Sex is not insurance against abandonment, even if you're terrific in bed
• Sex will not shore up a shaky ego.

OBSESSIONS AND COMPULSIONS

HAVE YOU EVER FOUND yourself checking that you've really locked your front door even though you've just checked it? Or noticed the same thought spinning round and round your mind, which you couldn't seem to suppress? Most of us fall prey to obsessive thoughts or compulsive behavior at some point in our lives: The question is, at what level do they become a problem?

Repetitive cycles

Obsessions and compulsions are often linked but, in general, obsessions relate to thoughts and feelings, with the same thought, word, or phrase persistently repeating itself in a person's mind, while compulsions relate to actions—washing one's hands after touching anything, for example. There is no fixed point at which professional help is necessary. Some obsessions or compulsions are not seen as harmful, such as the scientist who feels driven to work all night on tests to find a cure for cancer, or the art collector obsessed by a particular artist. Others are mundane and might not seem like compulsions at all, like the woman who carefully arranges her things on her dressing table before going out.

Taken to extremes, however, any of these examples could cause unhappiness. The woman who can't go out until her brushes and make-up jars are perfectly arranged, and who takes hours achieving a "perfect" position, will have less and less time and energy to devote to more rewarding activities. This restricted life may leave her feeling powerless and frustrated, and could also damage her self-esteem. If she doesn't recognize the "pay-off" her behavior gives her—that is, what the compulsive actions allow her to avoid—then the problem is likely to become worse. For example, her staying at home rearranging her things might be a way of

avoiding confronting something she finds scary or difficult—such as meeting people or facing new situations or challenges.

Facing the problem

Obsessions or compulsions are a problem when they restrict a person from enjoying a full life and realizing his or her potential. They may prevent the person from working, or from forming relationships. Obsessive-compulsive behavior is often closely allied to depression and anxiety, and can be part of a larger mental health problem. Fortunately, there has been much research into these problems, and psychiatrists, psychologists, and behavioral therapists can now often help people free themselves of these limiting problems very effectively.

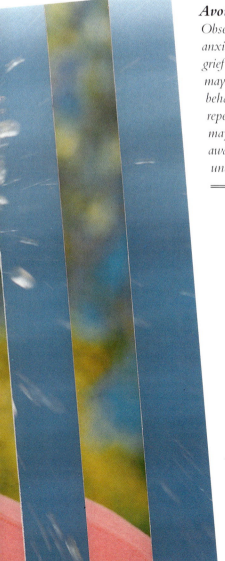

Avoiding feelings

Obsessions often stem from anxiety, such as suppressed grief or fear of change. They may develop into compulsive behavior—for example, repeated hand-washing may be a way of "washing away" feelings that seem unacceptable or dangerous.

BREAKING PAST PATTERNS

It is possible to break a cycle of obsessive thoughts, particularly if you become attuned to possible danger signs before the problem has become deeply rooted. The following guidelines can help you prevent an obsession from developing.

• Are you anxious about something? Anxiety over life events, such as the birth of a baby or a house move, can start a chain of anxiety that leads to an obsession. Reduce anxiety by giving it an outlet rather than suppressing it; talk to someone you trust, and also give yourself time for relaxation.

• If you have obsessive thoughts, ask yourself "What is the worst thing that can happen?" For instance, if you worry obsessively that your house isn't clean enough, consider what is the real consequence of the dust? Write down the worst thing, such as "My friends and neighbors would think less of me." What does this tell you about yourself—perhaps that you cannot see your own worth, and have to rely on others' judgment of you?

• Obsessive thinkers are often pessimistic. For instance, fearing the car will break down is bound to mean you will be abandoned alone with no help. Break this stranglehold of negativity by listing all the positive outcomes that are just as likely, such as "My partner will go for help," "I can call the recovery service," or " I have the car serviced regularly, so a breakdown is unlikely."

• Obsessive thoughts can seem like hearing a tape playing over and over again in your head which you cannot switch off. Try giving the tape a new script, mentally replacing the old wording with a positive cycle or series of thoughts to help displace or drown out the negative, obsessive thoughts. Any time you hear the old thoughts returning, simply stop, breathe slowly and relax for a moment, then consciously activate your new tape.

• If a friend or partner shows signs of developing an obsession, you will need to be sympathetic and encouraging. Try to avoid angry responses, and help the sufferer to seek help. Ask your physician about local self-help groups or therapists.

CURING COMPULSIVE BEHAVIOR

Compulsive behavior, such as repeated, uncontrolled checking, is more than just an irritating nuisance that wastes a person's time and energy. Often, it stems from a deep-rooted problem that will remain unresolved for as long as the compulsion is used as a way of masking it. Compulsive hand-washing, for example, sometimes occurs after a death, perhaps providing the sufferer a way of shedding or "washing away" painful feelings of grief, loss, or guilt.

Psychoanalysis has often been used to treat these problems, particularly when they are allied to more serious underlying disorders such as chronic depression, but many compulsions can be helped by behavior therapy. In contrast to psychoanalysis, which aims to treat the underlying cause of the problem, behavior therapy tackles the symptoms of the problem—that is, it works directly at altering the way the sufferer handles the compulsion.

The causes of compulsion

The origins of compulsive behavior lie in a person's need to allay anxiety. In many cases, the compulsion proceeds through a series of stages:

1. The person feels anxious, often over a specific event, such as the death or serious illness of someone close. Less easily definable feelings may also give rise to discomfort, including those caused by a generally unhappy childhood. The person feels totally unable to deal with this anxiety, and tries to suppress the memory or thought.

2. The buried feeling seems to disappear, and the person may initially experience a sense of relief. But, because the emotional pain remains suppressed and has not been aired, the unconscious mind seeks to bring the problem to the surface, and it manifests itself in compulsive behavior, such as hand-washing or checking.

3. The compulsive behavior starts to become noticeably bothersome or intrusive. Although the behavior may be annoying to the sufferer, it feels more under control than the frightening, real emotion—such as grief or anger—that the person should be feeling, and therefore the behavior serves to mask the chaos of confused emotion beneath the compulsion.

4. The compulsion acts as a locked door against the unhappiness within. While mental and emotional energy is diverted toward, say, hand-washing, the greater anxiety has no room to be felt or expressed.

5. The compulsion continues as a cycle of behavior. The unconscious has frozen anxiety, leading to more compulsion, which blocks the real fear within, so the anxiety is not expressed, and the compulsion remains.

Getting help

Compulsive behavior can be helped by counseling or psychotherapy, which can be very effective in dealing with problems or long-suppressed feelings that have caused the compulsion. Grief, anger, guilt, fear, self-loathing, and other strong feelings can be safely explored in psychotherapy.

Behavior therapy can provide a gradual release from the compulsion and its dominance of a person's life. Once the energy that has been diverted into maintaining the compulsion is released, this can provide a great sense of freedom, and enable the person to initiate change and take control of his or her life. The full force of the suppressed anxiety can also be released and, at first, this may be painful, or even be experienced as a backward step. But if the person is given support and help at this stage, he or she can work at regaining a more balanced approach to life.

Making progress

Behavior therapy commonly uses a gradually staged approach to free sufferers from their compulsive behavior. For example:

1. Sufferers are asked to assess their problem—for example, how long do they spend washing/dusting/checking, etc.? They are asked to rate their anxiety levels and how these relate to the time spent over the compulsion, and also how they would feel if interrupted.

2. Each level of anxiety is linked to a specific part of the compulsion. For example, a sufferer might find washing his or her hands in the bathroom at home involves less anxiety than washing them in a public washroom. Gradually, the behavior is confronted; the individual tackles the least upsetting situation, and learns how to cope with it with the benefit of support.

People may also be taught a technique called "self-limiting." This may be as simple as setting a limit to the amount of time spent indulging the compulsion. Or a more complex set of limits may be advised, with self-monitoring of thoughts as well as behavior changes.

3. As the compulsive person gains confidence, he or she moves up through a personal scale of difficulty. Eventually, he or she can cope with situations that once would have been agonizing. This graded approach—known as "habituation"—works effectively for many forms of compulsive disorder.

Looking ahead

If a compulsion has taken control of your life, it is vital to take action to free yourself. A compulsion is unlikely to fade away of its own accord, and, left to its own devices, is likely to get worse. The first step to overcoming a compulsion is to acknowledge that it exists. It is not a weakness to accept that you need help for this kind of difficulty, any more than it would be to see a physician if you sprained your ankle. Ask your family doctor if there is a self-help group locally you can attend or find out if your nearest hospital has a behavioral therapy unit (see also "Getting Help," pp. 136–137).

Identifying the cause
Once the underlying cause is known, it can be separated out from the compulsion, allowing the sufferer to work through the problem and tackle the compulsion separately.

CHAPTER FOUR

FINDING YOUR OWN POWER

EARLIER CHAPTERS may have helped you to identify some areas of your life over which you would like more control. But are there problem areas that you are deliberately ignoring because you feel their solution lies far beyond your power—with your boss, your partner, even with your circumstances, such as where you live? This chapter encourages you to take responsibility for every single area of your life. Even if you are unable to control some elements directly, you can learn to master your response to events, to great effect.

The key to self-control is finding and using your inner power. To do this you need to build up a positive image of yourself, which means identifying and learning to accept the real "you," with all your strengths and weaknesses. In this way you can build on your strong points and prepare yourself more effectively for any difficult situations you may encounter.

For many people perhaps the most useful life skill they can acquire is assertiveness. Being assertive means taking control of your emotions so that you are able to handle all types of difficult situations, such as confrontation, opposition, or put-downs. To find your own power you also need to discover what you actually think of yourself. "Change Your Self-talk" on pages 122-123 shows you how to do this by tuning into your inner voice, or "self-talk." You may be surprised at the negative views about yourself that your inner voice reveals. If you can eliminate these you will be able to achieve a fundamental shift in attitude and discover a more positive and effective you.

Presenting a relaxed and confident appearance to the world is vital to our feelings of self-worth. With this aim in mind, we offer "Calm Your Nerves" on pages 114-115, and "Control Your Own Image" on pages 118-119—both features that will help you to achieve greater poise and self-assurance.

An integral part of life that many people find particularly frightening is change. But change should be a positive force in your life, and is much easier to handle if you are flexible. In your relationships, too, change may seem frightening, but this should not stop you from facing and dealing with unsatisfactory situations. We offer advice on how to construct a plan of action that will help you achieve a healthy interdependence in your relationships. Finally, we look at the later years, and how you can grow in wisdom at every stage of your life.

ONCE YOU BEGIN TO ADDRESS AN ISSUE IN YOUR LIFE YOU WILL VERY QUICKLY FEEL THE EFFECTS. THIS SENSE OF ACHIEVEMENT WILL THEN GIVE YOU NEW ENERGY AND CONFIDENCE.

THE SECRET OF EMPOWERMENT

THE SECRET of real personal strength is believing in yourself— in knowing that, no matter what your circumstances, you are a capable, loving, and lovable human being. Great wealth, an adoring partner, or a fantastic job, may make you feel good, or in control of your life, but if you invest everything you are in externals, there is a real danger that your emotional well-being could suffer if a key aspect of your life were to suddenly disappear.

Some people confuse self-empowerment with being self-willed and always wanting to have your own way: It is not. Forcing people to do things that they are not happy with is a bad solution for everyone—it causes resentment all round and you will make yourself many enemies. Real personal strength springs from a clear and honest evaluation of yourself and the world around you. Amongst other things, it means that you will not be afraid of doing whatever it takes to find the best solution for everyone, that you are able to handle criticism constructively, and that you are open to learning new things. Problems will occur in your life over which you may feel you have no control, but from a position of personal strength you will be able to minimize the distress such problems cause you, and will be better able to decide on the best course of action.

Learn to be yourself

The main obstacles to feeling the power to "be yourself" are lack of self-esteem and self-confidence. The first steps to combating these are to become aware how much a sense of low self-worth forms an ever-present undercurrent in your daily life, and to confront your lack of self-confidence in specific situations. One of the most effective tools that you can use to build up your self-esteem is assertive behavior, as opposed to passive or aggressive behavior. This is looked at in more detail on pages 112–113.

EXERCISING CONTROL

Try these two exercises. They will help identify the areas in which you could be more effective.

• Your assertiveness record

Think carefully about what happened yesterday, or today, both at home and at work. Write down the details of when and where you felt you were in control of situations, no matter how important or unimportant they may seem.

What were your feelings? Also think about when, where, and how you behaved assertively. Did you give out any positive messages and receive positive feedback from people? Now list the ways in which you think you could have improved your performance.

• Role-playing

Ask a friend to "role-play" a situation with you, such as returning a faulty garment and meeting a wall of resistance from the shop assistant. Then swap roles.

How did you do? If you found yourself in the customer role becoming upset, indignant, and inarticulate, read over the first two points under "Boost your personal power." Discuss how you could integrate these skills, then try the role-play again.

Boost your personal power

There are ways that you can begin to build on your self-esteem straight away:

• **Think and behave positively**. Decide what you want, state it clearly, and stick with it. Begin to think of yourself as a strong person. If you think in this way you will find that others will treat you as confident and strong, and this in turn will help you to change your self-image.

• **Communicate positively and assertively.** This is a skill that will help you to feel on top of almost any situation. Make eye contact, and approach people with a confident, warm handshake. Use your tone of voice and body language to your advantage. Speak clearly and steadily rather than in a loud, overbearing voice, or with a shaky, uncertain one. Do you fidget, or have any nervous gestures (see also pp. 74-75)? Practice suppressing these unattractive habits and you will be amazed at the results—not only will others take you more seriously, but you will feel much calmer and stronger, too. Choose assertive language such as, "I'll enjoy finding out how to do that," rather than "I'll never be able to do that, I've never done it before." Use the word "I" in conversation. This isn't necessarily self-centered; it is a way of taking responsibility for what you say and think and raising your own profile.

Release your inner potential

Once you come to terms with the real you and the real world, you will be able to operate from a position of true strength and confidence.

• **Learn to relax.** Physical tension and mental stress feed off each other, and if you are agitated in any way, you will feel vulnerable rather than in control. Whenever you are feeling tense, take a few minutes out for some long, deep breaths. Concentrate on drawing in new strength as you breathe in, and letting go of tensions as you breathe out. Identify parts of your body that often feel strained—back, neck, and shoulders are common areas—and try consciously tensing them and relaxing them as you breathe in and out. Think about how you breathe normally. If you make an effort to breathe deeply and evenly rather than shallowly, it will soon become a habit, and you will feel much calmer.

• **Stop putting things off.** "I'll get around to changing my life after I've painted the bedroom/when I get back from holiday/as soon as I've finished this project at work," can easily escalate into "I'll get around to painting the bedroom after I've...." Delay makes you feel small and powerless; not only are you not achieving your long-term goals, but there always seems to be a mounting list of short-term tasks that aren't getting done either. If deep down you feel a course of action is right, do it now—you will feel enormously empowered by the sheer act of doing. From time to time, dare yourself to be spontaneous, to act on your intuition, or to make the first move—otherwise you could wait forever for conditions to be right.

• **Take time for yourself.** Making space to do the things you really want to do doesn't mean you are being selfish—there is no rule that says you always have to put everyone else's wishes and needs before your own. Learn to say no, directly and pleasantly. You need your own time to learn about yourself. Don't worry that this might lead to self-obsession, quite the opposite—it's hard to be interested in the world around you if you feel that you never have enough time for yourself.

You can derive the best kind of power, a power that isn't selfish or manipulative, from truly knowing and being yourself. And once you feel the strength of your own personal, permanent support system, you can start to take control.

DO YOU FEEL POWERLESS?

Feeling as if you have no control in the face of your emotions, or in your dealings with other people, creates considerable stress. Powerlessness also generates feelings of anger and frustration similar to those experienced by children in a world dominated by adults. This questionnaire will help you identify the situations in which you feel impotent. For each scenario, decide how powerless you think you would feel in similar circumstances: score one if you would feel totally powerless, two if you would feel moderately powerless, or three if you would be able to take some degree of control. Then turn to page 140 for an analysis of your score.

Relationships

1. My partner's mother is interfering and bossy. She constantly criticizes the way the house is run and our daughter is being brought up. My partner adores her, thinks she can do no wrong, and wants to invite her on our family holiday.

2. I love my partner, but occasionally I would like the opportunity to go away to visit my old college friends on my own. When I try to discuss this, my partner becomes upset and angry.

3. My teenage son makes it quite clear that he resents my new partner, and they have frequent rows. I love them both and find these outbursts both divisive and distressing.

4. My partner is very flirtatious. I've explained that such behavior makes me feel insecure and that I can't understand why he/she would want to hurt me, but he/she insists I'm overreacting.

Work

1. My new boss has begun to leave a lot of day-to-day decision-making to me, even though I have never had any real responsibility before.

2. The firm where I have worked for years is introducing a number of new computer systems to increase productivity and I fear these may put my job in jeopardy.

3. My company gives yearly staff appraisals. My supervisor is inefficient and disorganized, and this makes it hard for me to do my job properly, and I'm not sure if I should mention this to anyone.

4. My boss expects me to do his/her shopping and personal errands. I'm a trained secretary, and these tasks are not part of my job specification.

Daily life

1. I have a secure job, yet my bank manager has refused my request for a small loan without offering any explanation.

2. I suffer from the debilitating condition ME (myalgic encephalomyelitis), but my new doctor is unwilling to accept the diagnosis and treats me as though I'm a time-waster and a hypochondriac.

3. I suspect that the contractors I've hired to build my conservatory extension are cheating me.

4. Although I have explained repeatedly that my daughter suffers from dyslexia, her teacher continues to label her as stupid and lazy.

Social life

1. My partner's job requires us to attend a great many social functions. At these occasions, the conversation often turns to subjects I know nothing about, although everyone else seems to have an informed opinion.

2. Since my divorce, I have to attend parties and receptions on my own. Often, these occasions involve walking into a roomful of strangers.

3. My son married a girl from a wealthier and more influential family than ours. When we all get together, her parents often make reference to this.

4. When, at a party or stag night, a stripper performs in an explicit way, I feel like walking out, even though everyone else seems to find it very amusing.

The world

1. Day after day, the news media seem to be dominated by increasingly distressing reports of torture, starvation, illness, and murder.

2. I am increasingly convinced that our very existence as a species is being threatened by the greenhouse effect and the gradual destruction of the environment.

3. Although recession and unemployment are on the increase, all contemporary politicians appear to be inherently self-interested, dishonest, and inflexible.

4. Violence, crime, racism, and poverty are rife in our society. Our cities are full of homeless teenagers, and old people are not given any care or the respect they deserve.

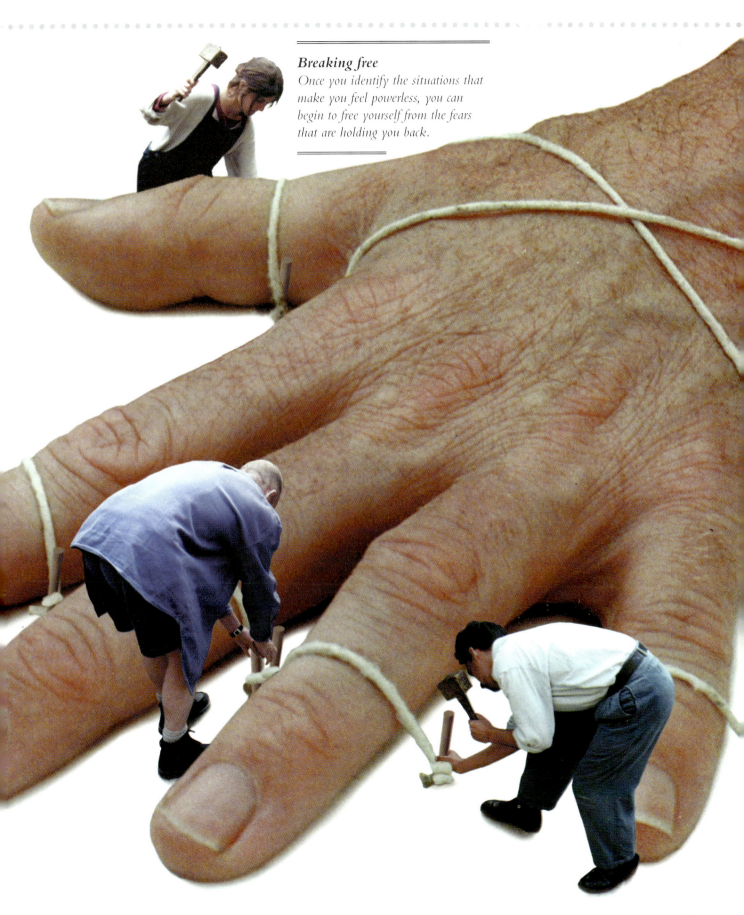

Breaking free
Once you identify the situations that make you feel powerless, you can begin to free yourself from the fears that are holding you back.

POWER GAMES

MANY OF US have experienced the feeling at some time or other that the way we live our lives is being dictated by other people. Employers, bank managers, bureaucrats, doctors, even friends or partners are all individuals we are likely to see as having some kind of power over us. It is also tempting to attribute to these others skills, talents, or even luck that we feel we do not possess.

Although many of our feelings of powerlessness probably stem from childhood experiences, when we were often helpless to control our circumstances, fortunately as adults there are a number of techniques that we can use to build up our self-esteem and confidence—the very qualities that will help to redress the balance of power.

Assess the opposition

When it comes to issues of power—whether real or emotional—that are giving you problems, try to confront your own perception by asking yourself whether you are reacting, or overreacting, to the situation you are actually experiencing, or whether, rather, your reaction is a consequence of experiences you have had in the past. What power do these people actually have, what is at the root of your feeling of subordination and, most importantly, is it your own lack of confidence and self-esteem that allows you to invest in them qualities that are, in fact, illusory?

You may well find, on closer examination, that many of the people you believe have control over your life possess no real power other than that with which you provide them. If possible, go through your responses with another person whose perspective on life you consider to be well-balanced—he or she may cast a useful light on areas of difficulty for you.

Face reality

No one likes confrontation, and we all have an understandable tendency to want to avoid people and situations that we find uncomfortable, but it is much more constructive to learn to deal with them.

An important step is to get a clear view of the balance of power between you and the other person. Remember, you may be investing other people with more power over your life than they really have, or want. Your feelings of powerlessness may also be fueled by misapprehensions about yourself. Much of the basis for these doubts lies in our childhood, when we may acquire a belief that our behavior requires constant approval from others, and any experience of that approval not being forthcoming threatens our self-esteem. Instead of just feeling that we have *done* something bad or stupid, we believe that we *are* bad or stupid, that we are not only unloved, but unlovable.

A great deal can also be accomplished by recognizing and acknowledging your own needs and requirements when facing what you in reality know to be the unreasonable demands made on you by others, whether it be an employer, friend, or even child. In many ways it can appear to be easier just to accept these demands rather than have to pay the emotional price of refusing them. However, continuing this behavior may well have the effect of establishing further habitual responses in those people with whom you interact— the more you say yes, the more frequent and exploitative their demands are likely to become. Make time for yourself to look calmly and rationally at what is being demanded of you and whether you want to give it.

Another useful exercise is to analyze your response to criticism. If you always take criticism as a personal attack, there are several ways to counteract this tendency. You could try to evaluate for yourself the validity and truth of the criticism. If you judge it to be valid, acknowledge it both to yourself and to the other person, but in as positive a way as possible. For example, "Yes, I understand what you say about my behavior, but it is how I work best; however, I will note what you say." If, on the other hand, you sincerely believe the criticism to be untrue or not valid, respond immediately and with as much self-assurance (but not aggression) as you can muster.

Feel your own power

If you always compare yourself with others and feel that you don't measure up, try to challenge this perspective by consciously adopting a more positive view of yourself and your abilities. Bring to your attention those parts of yourself that you like and the things that you know you can do well. Hold them in your mind, and in your imagination practice confronting those situations and those people that would normally frighten you. Carefully note the differences that this "dress rehearsal" makes in your feelings about both them and yourself.

It is not conceit to hold yourself in good esteem if it is the result of impartial self-examination and an acceptance of those qualities and abilities that you can find inside yourself.

"Please, sir"

Many of us have continued as adults to experience ambivalent childhood feelings toward authority figures—on the one hand wanting to be "teacher's pet," and on the other resenting the apparent power they wield over our lives.

Be positive

An assertive approach goes a long way to ensuring a more positive outcome in dealings with others— more details are given on pages 112–113. Assertive behavior is often confused with aggressive behavior, which is, as a rule, socially unacceptable. Thus many people choose to accept powerlessness rather than confront a problem.

BE RESPONSIBLE

When things go wrong, an immediate reaction may be to blame others for the situations in which we find ourselves. When we are struggling to cope, we are often tempted to rely on other people to sort out our problems for us. However, allowing other people to have a degree of responsibility over our lives —whether real or imaginary—means that we are not in control.

Blaming others

Consider the following situations, and ask yourself how you would behave:

During an argument, Sue finds the behavior of her partner so unacceptable that she completely loses her temper and walks out of the house, slamming the door with such aggression that it shatters the glass. She accuses her partner: *"I couldn't help it, you made me lose my temper."*

Chris has to make a presentation at work, but it doesn't go down well and he gets complaints from his colleagues. He blames it on his boss: *"It's his fault for not giving me enough time to prepare properly."*

Jill's car breaks down in the middle of a journey and she finds the reason is that it is overdue for a service. She believes it is the garage's fault: *"They should have told me the service was due."*

Harry gets a threatening letter from his building society because he has fallen behind with his mortgage repayments. He blames them: *"They should never have let me take on such high repayments."*

Robert's wife is taken into hospital and he finds it difficult to cook himself proper meals. He blames her: *"It's her fault—she never lets me in the kitchen."*

Angela's husband has left her and she finds herself getting behind in paying bills and her bank account becoming overdrawn. She holds him responsible: *"It's his fault—he always insisted on looking after money matters."*

Julia's boyfriend is away for the weekend. Her house lights go out and she can't change the fuse. She blames her boyfriend: *"It's not my fault I can't do it—he never showed me how."*

Sally insists on offering her friend advice when it is not asked for, and her friend crossly tells her so. Instead of acknowledging that she should have minded her own business, Sally reproaches her with: *"I was only trying to help."*

Start to take charge

How did you fare in the above situations? Did you empathize with some or all of the responses given, or on the whole did you find yourself disagreeing with them? Perhaps you find it easy to take responsibility in certain situations, but difficult in others, reacting automatically in certain ways. When we start blaming others, it can often be the result of unproductive thinking—"It's not fair," "Life shouldn't be like this," "I shouldn't have to feel uncomfortable." A tendency always to blame other people for your own life also reflects a lack of awareness of their rights as well as your own. Among these is the right to fail, and to learn and grow as a result of your failures.

Remember, too, that your emotions are under your control—you are the person who makes yourself upset or angry, no one else. Using emotional manipulation to make others feel guilty for your reactions, telling them they made you feel like that, denies your ability to take responsibility.

Responsible attitude

Accepting responsibility when appropriate is self-empowering. Take Angela, for example. She decided eventually to stop blaming her husband and to take practical steps toward financial responsibility. She got professional advice on how best to handle her money matters, and drew up a realistic financial plan. Angela discovered that she could keep within her budget—something she never thought possible. She found herself enjoying her new-found independence, and she gained confidence in her ability to handle other difficult situations.

"Passing the buck"
At times, it is all to easy to try to shift the blame onto someone else for our own difficulties and mishaps in life.

Are You Assertive?

Have you ever vowed to be more assertive—perhaps after a confrontation with someone in which you did not achieve the results you wanted? But do you know exactly what this entails? Being assertive is not just about being forceful and getting your own way, as we saw on pages 104–105; it is about learning to understand your feelings and expressing them clearly, honestly, and respectfully. To assert yourself effectively, and to take control of a situation, it is important to have a positive attitude toward yourself and *others*.

Few people behave assertively all the time. On the other hand, many people *never* behave assertively. For most of us there are situations that we find comfortable, and where it is easy to act assertively. Other situations—particularly confrontational ones—are less easy to deal with, however, and frequently result in one or both parties feeling upset and aggrieved.

Are you OK?

According to a branch of psychotherapy known as Transactional Analysis (TA), there are four main life "positions" that color everything we do: passive, aggressive, manipulative, and assertive. These can be used to categorize the way that people interact, based on the "transactions" they make with each other. Psychiatrist Thomas A. Harris, in his book *I'm OK—You're OK*, defines a transaction as "I do something to you and you do something back," and describes the positions thus:

• **I'm not OK—you're OK** A passive position that is characterized by low self-esteem
• **I'm not OK—you're not OK** A manipulative position in which a person feels negative about him- or herself
• **I'm OK—you're not OK** An aggressive stance in which negative feelings hide behind bravado
• **I'm OK—you're OK** An assertive stance in which a person feels positive about both themselves and others

These life positions develop early in childhood and stick with us for life. Fortunately, it is possible to change the three negative life views to the highly desirable fourth position: assertiveness. Try the following exercise—it will help you think about how and why you handle difficult situations in the way that you do.

Assess Yourself

Consider this situation. Instead of going away on vacation this summer, you are looking forward to recharging your batteries at home by reading, relaxing, and seeing friends. This will also save money, which is tight at the moment. Then your girlfriend rings and says that, as you had no plans, she has gone ahead and booked for you to go away on vacation with her. She has paid for the flights, but you will have to pay for some costly accommodation she has arranged. She knows how much you enjoy getting away, and felt that this would be a wonderful surprise treat. Which of the following best describes the way you would react?

A. You feel that you have no choice but to do what your girlfriend wants, despite disappointment that you can't do as you had planned, and great concern about your financial situation.

B. You don't tell your girlfriend how annoyed you are, but pay her back by telling her you can't go because you have made plans to go away with others.

C. You have a big row with your girlfriend and refuse to go on the holiday on principle. You feel happy that you are in control of your own life again.

D. You thank her for trying to sort out a nice surprise for you, but explain clearly what your plans are and why you want to stick to them. You suggest a night out together the following week.

A satisfactory outcome?

Which response did you choose? The descriptions below show how the responses fit into the four different categories of Transactional Analysis and may explain why you feel the way you do.

A. "I'm not OK—you're OK"

Your low self-esteem means you feel frightened that if you turn your girlfriend down, your relationship may be threatened. Your lack of self-confidence may even persuade you that your girlfriend's idea is bound to be a better, more interesting option than your own.

B. "I'm not OK—you're not OK"

Your problem is that you don't like yourself or others—your girlfriend's behavior is just typical of that of your thoughtless friends. You always suspect other people's motives, and this mistrust leads you into manipulative behavior.

C. "I'm OK—you're not OK"

You bury your lack of self-confidence behind an aggressive exterior, making yourself feel better in the short-term by comparing yourself with others and finding the other party lacking. In the long-term, however, the outcome leaves you feeling unsatisfied.

D. "I'm OK—you're OK"

You feel positive about yourself, others and the world around you. You manage to avoid being waylaid by false logic or emotional manipulation. Neither do you take any implied criticism personally. This leads to an outcome that is satisfactory for everyone.

CALM YOUR NERVES

Whether it's speaking in public, or dealing with difficult people, there are many situations where to be at your most effective, you need to keep calm and stay in control. Although you may fear anxiety and even panic, by using calming techniques you will be able to get yourself into a more relaxed state.

Imaging success

Picturing yourself successfully achieving your desired frame of mind is a particularly effective technique—one that athletes use to psych themselves up before competing in an event. They think about the race in great detail—right down to the feeling of what it will be like to burst through the tape at the end of the race. By visualizing victory, they can increase the flow of adrenaline and access a highly charged state before the race has even begun. For many top athletes, this part of the build-up to an event is an important and integral part of their training.

Panic stations?

However stressful your life might be, picturing yourself in situations where you would be calm and relaxed will bring those feelings into the present.

Studies have shown that as well as using positive mental images to increase performance during strenuous activities, the same method can also be used to reduce stress and anxiety by recalling calming experiences, such as lying in the sun or taking in some idyllic scenery. It is important, however, that the appropriate state of mind be recalled depending on what atmosphere you want to re-create. It would be of little benefit to someone about to participate in a highly physical activity to access the feelings of sitting in a comfortable armchair. Similarly, if you are trying to calm down and relax, it is counter-productive to access states when you were very excited.

Visualization in practice

Mary became very anxious every time she was called in to speak with her boss. She automatically assumed that he was about to criticize her, and began to shake and breathe heavily. Realizing that this was hampering her ability to deal with her boss, she decided to visualize how she could control her nerves. Telling herself "I am an efficient, capable woman," she pictured herself going to her boss's office, smiling at him, and him praising her work. She imagined exactly how she would feel. The next time she saw her boss, he complemented her, and said he would give her more responsibility.

Don, meanwhile, was very anxious in large groups of people. He avoided social situations where large groups were present, but he realized that he was depriving himself of rewarding experiences and of meeting many new people who would enhance his life. Relaxing deeply in a chair, he talked positively to himself, saying, "I enjoy meeting new people. Parties are fun." Repeating this over and over again, he visualized himself chatting to groups of people and being in a large, noisy party. When he actually went to one, he found that his dread had gone, and he enjoyed himself.

Breathing techniques

One of the easiest ways to calm your nerves is through controlling your breathing. This can be particularly helpful in managing the effects of panic attacks. A common symptom is hyperventilation—rapidly breathing in from the upper chest, resulting in too much oxygen and insufficient carbon dioxide coming into the body. This makes you feel as though you cannot breathe, and, in turn, you take even more rapid breaths. Following this, there may be tension in the upper body, dizziness, and shaking.

There are simple techniques to control this. First, monitor your breathing throughout the day, placing your hand on your diaphragm. Then, develop your skills in holding your breath. Do not do this for the first time when you are in a state of anxiety, but practice holding your breath for a few seconds after you have completely exhaled. As a quick calming technique, hold a paper bag or cupped hands over your mouth and breathe as slowly as you can. This will normalize your breathing pattern and help you to calm down.

RELAX!

The following methods of calming yourself down have worked for many people. If they don't work for you at first, it is important to keep trying: You have already learned how to be anxious in various situations—so, conversely, it is quite possible for you to learn how to calm down.

• Use positive language. Don't say, "I want to be less stressed"; instead say, "I am now calmer," or "I am totally relaxed."

• Get yourself into a relaxed state by using deep breathing techniques. Breathe in slowly through your nose, and then out again slowly through your mouth.

• When you are calm, clench and then let go of each group of muscles, starting with your toes, and working across your entire body.

• Picture yourself doing something that you enjoy, which makes you feel calm and relaxed.

• When you start thinking of that relaxing and calming event, think about it in as much detail as you possibly can. Remember to take note not only of how you felt, but of how you looked and sounded as well. Provide yourself with the most minute details of the experience so that you can recall it as fully as possible.

• Practice. The more often you use these self-calming techniques, the easier and more effective they will become.

DEALING WITH PUT-DOWNS

A put-down is never constructive criticism—its object is to try to hurt and humiliate the recipient. More often than not, it catches you completely off guard, leaving you too shocked to formulate a proper response. But everyone is subjected to put-downs at some point—the trick is to know how to deal with them. Put-downs are power-games, designed to increase the power of the person giving them and to decrease your own. Some put-downs are easier to handle than others—being hurt by someone you respect is much harder to deal with than being patronized by someone you don't.

Responding effectively

The first step toward dealing with put-downs is to understand why people use them. Those who habitually put down other people tend to be very insecure, and have to make other people look small in order to bolster up their own self-confidence. In example three in the box below, the plump acquaintance has a vested interest in making you feel small. People whose approach is patronizing may often seem to be successful—but internally they are still struggling. It is likely that the work colleague in example one feels threatened by a young and enthusiastic workmate.

There are a number of different practical strategies for dealing with put-downs. Everyone knows the situation where he or she lies awake formulating clever ripostes to put-downs—things that didn't spring to mind at the time. This feeling can be even stronger when you don't realize that someone is putting you down until afterward.

One assertive technique is to ask the person exactly what they mean. In example two, for instance, you could ask your friend what he's

---

WHAT WOULD YOU DO?

So how do you cope? Look at these three situations, and consider how you would handle them in order to best maintain your self-respect and confidence.

1. You have just started in your first job. A particular colleague, who has been hostile and unhelpful from the start, one day picks up a letter you have written and says in a loud, arrogant voice, "So you're a graduate of the University of Incompetence. Everyone knows that the date goes above the address."
a) Seething with anger, you reply: "If you're so clever how come no one else has noticed."
b) You behave as though the comment was intended to be helpful and say: "Thank you for bringing that detail to my attention. If you have any other pointers to give me I'd be grateful."
c) Feeling utterly humiliated you rush to the toilet and burst into tears.

2. A friend of yours is broke and in desperate need of employment. To do him a favor you approach your boss (with whom you have an excellent working relationship) and suggest that your friend would be a good person to take on. After he has been working in the firm for a few weeks, your friend invites you to go out for a drink with him. As you settle down over your drinks, he says: "The boss thinks my handling of the new account is excellent. He said it was a relief to work with someone who has brains and initiative at last."
a) You snap angrily: "The only time you showed any brains and initiative was when you approached me to help you get a job."
b) You ignore the implications and reply: "If I hadn't expected you to be competent, I wouldn't have recommended you."
c) Feel hurt, but say only: "That's nice," then leave the bar at the first possible opportunity.

implying. People often back down at this point. In all of the situations outlined in the box below, you are being criticized in ways that are potentially hurtful. If you answer **a** to all the questions, you respond with barbed, clever comments, which come from your feelings of anger. If you answer **b**, you use reasoned comment, which disguises your feelings. If you answer **c**, then you tend to be overcome by feelings of hurt, and retreat into your pain.

Remember, the only person who can make you feel bad is yourself. When you have been the subject of a put-down, the wisest course of action is not to allow yourself to be overtaken by pain or anger or to react in a way that leaves the person believing their remarks have worked. Respond rationally and assertively, and know that you can rise above their comments.

3. You have a long-standing acquaintance who over the years has grown rather fat. At one meeting she says, "I found a photograph of you at Bill and Caroline's wedding. You look so young I can hardly believe it was only taken three years ago."
a) You give her your brightest smile and retort: "Funnily enough I came across an old photograph of you, too. I was absolutely amazed at how slim you used to be."
b) Repressing the urge to match put-down with put-down, you say: "We're all getting older."
c) You give her an icy stare—then pointedly ignore her for the rest of the evening.

Clowning about?
Put-downs can make you feel as if you've been made a fool of—but remember, it is the person who has made the hurtful remark who has a problem, not you. Knowing this will help you to stay assertive in the face of a verbal attack.

CONTROL YOUR OWN IMAGE

There is no doubt about it: appearance talks. The way we look says as much about our personality, status, class, and interests as our accents and opinions. Our choice of clothes and accessories, the way we use makeup (or not), the style of our hair, all contribute to the statement we are making about who and what we are.

How people see us

Cathy, a busy freelance journalist, had got into the habit of living in her baggy tracksuit and shapeless old cardigan. She rarely bothered with makeup and wore her hair scrunched into an untidy knot on the top of her head. She knew she had let herself go, but because she worked from home couldn't rouse herself to do anything about it. Then, one day, a neighbor with whom she was on nodding terms made a sympathetic reference to her being unemployed. Taken aback, Cathy suggested the woman had jumped to this conclusion because she was at home during the day. Her neighbor agreed, then added, "But it's also the way you look, dear." As a result, Cathy decided to take herself in hand. Her neighbor's comment reflected the image she was presenting to the world—and to herself—and she didn't like it.

Most of us have had experience of presenting an image we had not actively chosen. Remarks such as "You don't look like a career woman," or "I wouldn't have taken you for the serious type," give us a view of ourselves that is different from the one we see in our own mirrors. Being aware of this and learning to assess yourself objectively is an important step to taking positive control of your image.

Dressing appropriately

Taking charge of your image is not about becoming a fashion victim. Rather, it means having the confidence to choose the look you feel most reflects your tastes and individuality and knowing which outfit is suitable for which occasion. Different situations demand different styles of dress: Most of us would not consider

Look the part
Putting on the right outfit for the occasion—whether a work or social event—reinforces a positive self-image, and inspires others to have confidence in us.

jeans and boots appropriate wear for a cocktail party, for instance, and a tight skirt and heels would be ridiculous on a country walk. At different times we dress to conform, to seduce, to influence and impress, to create a favorable impact, and to boost our self-confidence. A man wearing a smart suit and tie, for example, indicates that he takes his standing in the world seriously. So does a woman wearing a crisply tailored outfit with an executive briefcase tucked under her arm.

Work clothes

Although dress codes at work are much less rigid than they used to be, there are still certain elements that have to be borne in mind. For many career women the need to indicate power and authority through their appearance is important. Indeed, there are those who maintain that looking successful is half the battle. It is certainly true that overtly feminine or sexy attire in the office works against a woman being taken seriously.

Although nowadays men's style outside work is under almost as much scrutiny as women's, they are judged less by what they wear at work. A basic work uniform of suit and tie is standard in many jobs, and many organizations have stricter dress codes for men than women. Everyone needs to remember that dress codes will vary in different work areas. What is right for a merchant bank will be totally wrong for a youth club. People who work across different spheres, such as counselors or consultants, should bear this in mind.

Grooming

Making a good impression is about the details of your appearance. This is particularly true in situations such as job interviews. Clean, brushed hair; subtle, well-applied makeup; clean fingernails, and polished shoes all help, whether or not you can afford to buy an expensive suit. None of these need cost much and other aspects of grooming can easily be worked around—even if you cannot afford to attend an expensive hairdresser every time, one good hair-cut will give cheaper hairdressers something to work from. Good posture is just as important to presenting a positive image to prospective employers as your clothes and hair.

The dress code
By choosing certain clothes, we can signal to others that we are serious or playful, active or relaxed, seductive or self-contained.

DIFFERENT STYLES

How much credence do you give to the well-known saying, "Clothes maketh the man"? Do you make assumptions about people's characters, their lifestyles, even their abilities, based on what they wear? Take a close look at the six people shown below. What do you think you can can tell about them by looking at them? Then examine the six pictures featured on the gallery walls. Do you find it easy to match a certain image to a particular person?

There are in fact no "right" answers to this exercise, although we give some likely interpretations on pages 140-141. Most of us can identify widely accepted "uniforms"—from the casual style of the student, to the formal attire of the office worker—but remember that what people choose to wear at any given time is only ever a part of who they are.

The appearance of things

During our lives we may take on or choose a number of roles— student, business person, professional, artist, parent. What you wear may be significant—accepted conventions of dress invite stereotyped assumptions about your character and abilities that may or may not be to your advantage.

CHANGE YOUR SELF-TALK

Each and every day of your life there is a continuous tape running inside your head, an internal voice programming the way you think about yourself. Sometimes you will be totally unaware of it. On other occasions, often when you least expect it, it will either spur you on or hold you back. What is your self-talk telling you? Is it saying that you are a competent, happy person, in control of your life? Or is it dragging you down with messages of worthlessness? If it is the latter, then it is up to you to change your stream of self-talk and put it firmly where it belongs—on your side.

The enemy within

The first thing to do is to get to know your enemy—your negative inner voice—as thoroughly as possible. Think of various episodes that took place today. Can you remember roughly what your self-talk was saying at certain significant points? In order for you to recognize your inner voice it will probably be helpful for you to write this down. If you keep some kind of "self-talk" diary, you will be able to spot patterns emerging and will no doubt see all too clearly how a trail of negative messages only ever leads to a negative outcome. You will be surprised when you discover how often, at certain crucial moments, your negative voice has held you back from making the best of an opportunity.

Now that you know when and where your negative voice is at its most active, you can start to tutor it to change its approach to a positive, encouraging one. For example, you may have seen that your voice is mostly positive, but becomes negative when faced with, for example, taking part in sport. When you next participate ·in a sporting activity, try repeating some of the following types of messages continuously to yourself:
• I am perfectly capable at playing the game.
• It really doesn't matter how good I am, as long as I enjoy myself.
• Lots of other people aren't very skilled, but they still join in with fun and enthusiasm, and brighten up the experience for everyone.

Direct your inner voice
To be in charge of your life, you need to tell your inner voice what you want it to say, and refuse to accept any of the negative messages that it may try to give you.

Opening up the dialogue

Once you have identified your negative voice, and feel that you know it only too well, you could employ role-playing techniques and try having a conversation with it. Give it some kind of visual appearance and try imagining that it is sitting in the chair opposite you. Or you could perhaps visualize it as a "talking head" on the TV. You might even try giving a close friend a character briefing on your negative voice and asking him or her to play-act the role. Now question your inner voice on what it thinks about a range of different matters, and argue with it constructively, putting a positive, encouraging view forward every time.

Once you start to disassociate yourself from your negative self-talk, you will find that it will become much less ingrained. Also, talking out loud often has the power to clarify matters much more effectively than hours of silent thought. Put yourself in the position of someone criticizing you, and the comments will sound increasingly untrue and worthless.

Encourage yourself

Your long-term goal should be to replace your negative voice with a positive one—a fundamental shift in attitude. Combining these types of exercises with simply repeating positive statements about yourself out loud will soon start to change the nature of both your subconscious and conscious thoughts.

These in turn will affect the way your mind and body behave. If you are constantly telling your body that it is weak, ill, or clumsy, it will be. On the other hand, telling yourself that you are healthy and exactly the right weight will put you on the way to being there.

Other ways to change your internal messages are to write down examples of positive self-talk wherever you will see them frequently—such as on the bathroom mirror, the fridge, or above your desk. Self-hypnosis audio or video tapes, which give you a series of subconscious positive messages, often based around a particular subject such as smoking or relationships, can also be beneficial, giving you positive messages when you are in a deeply relaxed state.

A positive outlook
A flourishing inner self will develop more naturally when it has been well directed and its negative talk has been quietened.

EXPAND YOUR HORIZONS

Our negative self-talk thrives on narrow, small-minded, and petty patterns of thought. If you expand the limits of your thoughts, you will find the meaner little ones beginning to disappear. Make sure that you work hard on making your life as full of variety as possible, and stop it from running along a single track such as your job. Try to make your mind reach outward to matters outside your own daily preoccupations. This might mean exercising it on political, environmental, or spiritual concerns if they interest you, or it might simply mean doing some local voluntary work, babysitting for neighbors, or organizing a special anniversary treat for relatives—even just writing letters to far-flung friends. You may say that you can't spare the time for these things, but just ten minutes each day spent thinking about

something or somebody else will make all the difference to your mental outlook. The nasty little voice that chatters on ceaselessly with limiting thoughts will gradually be replaced with a warm, outgoing, expansive voice telling you to go ahead and get all you can out of life.

Making tracks
To make your self-talk more positive you must avoid having a one-track mind. You should expand your thoughts to cover a broad spectrum of interests.

MAKING LIFE CHANGES

FROM THE MOMENT we are born until we die, our lives are subject to change. No area of our life remains untouched by change. In work, relationships, family, finances, health, personal development, change alters our lives, our circumstances, our behavior, and the way we see the world.

The threat of the new

Change, even positive change, can be very difficult to handle. Many of us enjoy the sense of security that comes from things being familiar. Change can make us feel anxious, threatened, or powerless, particularly if we are having to respond to changes initiated by others. Even when the change is a positive one, or one we have anticipated or planned, such as getting married or starting a new job, it may be hard to adjust, and we may hanker for the old, familiar life.

Certain changes are almost inevitable—such as our first day at school, leaving home, turning 40, becoming a grandparent. These staging posts are best regarded as an integral part of life. We can then learn from them and enjoy them, using them as part of the way we make changes in our lives, rather than simply being swept along by them or battling against them.

Choosing to change

Many of the primary changes in our lives are ones we choose to make—forming relationships, starting a family, moving house, and so on. Sometimes, there comes a point when we make the decision to change; in other cases, the change seems to happen by itself, but when we look back we realize that we did take action to make it happen.

Flexibility is vitally important; making major changes often has a knock-on effect in other areas of your life. You cannot expect to have a baby, for example, and still carry on your life in exactly the same way as you did before. The fact that nothing lasts forever seems impossible to young lovers; if they then have a child, their whole lives will change—they will have less time and money for themselves, but reading their child a bedtime story may bring as much joy as the headiness of being in love. When you are planning major life changes, spend some time considering the implications for the other strands of your life: Ask yourself how the change might affect your relationship, friendships, lifestyle, health, and finances, for example.

The process of adjustment

When you make key changes in your life, you will need to be patient with yourself. There are bound to be difficulties. You may find you feel panicky and want to revert to your old ways. This is only natural—it is hard to make fundamental changes and not have a single qualm. You may find it useful to make a list of the positive results that have ensued from your making the change, and to focus on how you might consolidate the change so that you can enjoy its benefits more fully.

CHANGING YOURSELF

There may be areas of your life that you would like to change. Acknowledging the need for change is an important step, but acknowledgment in itself does not create change. There is a gap between the intellectual recognition and actually altering the way you act or feel. Self-help books and personal development courses can offer practical help in implementing change.

There are also many simple techniques you can try that make a difference surprisingly quickly. For example, one approach is to try "acting as if...;" if you are habitually shy with strangers, you might try going to a party and "acting as if I am a relaxed and outgoing person." Beforehand, you could affirm your new image by picturing yourself at the party expressing yourself with confidence. How does it feel? What would your expression be? What would your posture be like? You could wear clothes in a different style, perhaps borrowing something from a friend whose confident qualities you would like to enjoy.

Once you go to the party and act in your new way, other people will be likely to be more relaxed with you in response to your changed manner. Gradually you will find yourself becoming more confident and relaxed without needing to act it.

First day

A mother knows that her child's first day at school may be traumatic, but that it is also a vital stepping stone in the child's life. All of us have to face up to, and learn from, such unavoidable changes in our lives.

STAGES OF CHANGE

Although some life changes take place virtually overnight, such as the arrival of a newborn or starting a new job, many changes involve a much more gradual, lengthy process. Recognizing the need for change may be just the first step; subsequent steps vary according to the type of change being made but may include: noticing the specific thoughts and behavior that hold you back, deciding that you are free to act differently in future, then actively working on changing your behavior, perhaps through practical exercises and personal resolve, or through some form of therapy. In *Beating the Comfort Trap*, Dr. Windy Dryden and Jack Gordon outline the following stages of change:

Stage 1: Change your thinking

By changing the way you think about things, you change the way you experience the world at large and everything that happens to you. For example, if you have a number of unreasonable or irrational expectations, they are extremely unlikely to be fulfilled, so you are bound to end up feeling disappointed, hard done by, and defeated. Many people irrationally believe that they should always feel completely at ease, which makes them highly intolerant of any frustration or emotional discomfort, and can result in an "If at first you don't succeed, give up" attitude.

Another irrational belief is that we must avoid emotional pain at all costs, and as a result we steer clear of potentially uncomfortable or difficult situations, instead of facing up to our fears and gaining in strength from the experience. We may also attempt to numb our emotions, or block ourselves from experiencing our feelings, by closing ourselves off from real joy and intimacy as we try to avoid feeling hurt or pain.

Stage 1 of the process involves acknowledging all of your self-defeating beliefs and expectations, and making a dedicated commitment to change these beliefs and expectations on a permanent basis. Assessing your interactions with other people, and how you felt and acted in certain situations in the past, will help you see where your expectations have had positive results and helped you to move forward and act effectively and, conversely, where they have restricted your ability to change and grow.

Taking the rough with the smooth
Realizing that life is not always a smooth trip helps you make steady progress toward the changes you want and overcome rough patches on the way.

Stage 2: Put the past behind you

We are all born with our own distinct personality traits, which are later modified to varying degrees by the influence of our family, society, and life experiences. A person from an unhappy background, however, will have far greater difficulty changing his or her irrational beliefs and expectations than someone whose home life was happy and nurturing, but whatever the circumstances, everyone has the capacity to think rationally, to take positive action, and to effect change.

To move on from any negative influences that featured in your past, you must decide to accept complete responsibility for running your own life, and resist the all too tempting desire to blame other people and external circumstances for your shortcomings. Be willing to be honest with yourself and to learn from the mistakes that you have made. You have to risk feeling uncomfortable as you move steadily away from the familiar, easy, but self-limiting, behavior of the past.

Stage 3: Build your resolve

In your pursuit of a happier and more fulfilled life, resolve and self-discipline are your greatest allies in the move to implement change. Having a steady resolve will help you to stick to your intentions, avoid being thrown off course by any irrelevant distractions or minor obstacles, and enable you to keep pushing forward to be the way you would really like to be.

If you feel your resolve tends to waver, it may be helpful to team up with another person with similar intentions for mutual support. You can use each other as a sounding board to discuss the changes you want to make, provide each other with constructive feedback on the way as you are making those changes, and give each other the moral support you will both need to help you through the tough patches. Having somebody around when you feel your resolve slipping can help you stay on course while you gradually become stronger.

Foundations for the future

If there are times when all this dedication to change feels like too much effort, ask yourself whether avoiding responsibility and clinging to myths of effortless rewards have ever helped you achieve what you really want. Change undoubtedly involves hard work—as do many other things we value most in life. To sustain you in the work and effort of building a better future, keep your sights set on the image of the life you want to have and the person you want to be.

ESCAPING THE CO-DEPENDENCY TRAP

___

Stay afloat
If you feel that your role in life is to rescue drowning partners, then you are pulling yourself under, too, and must make your escape.

___

One of the most damaging effects of constantly playing the "caretaker" role in relationships, always trying to sort out the other's life, is that you can easily become trapped in a situation that seems to offer no possibility for change—an endless cycle of unrealistically high hopes followed by crashing disappointments. Vast amounts of energy and time are spent hoping that the partner will change, if only you can help him or her enough. And all the while you're getting older and angrier. It may not be easy to escape this trap—but it *can* be done.

Addicted to helplessness

Gilly spent five years in a relationship with Philip just after his second marriage had crumbled, and his latest business venture, a restaurant, had failed and left him penniless. Feeling that he would benefit from her loving care and contacts in the catering world, Gilly moved him and his children in with her. She also persuaded a friend to give him a job. Gilly felt confident that she had set Philip up, and secure that he had a special place in his heart for her because she had turned his life around. Then she discovered that he was having an affair with a friend of hers. She put up with his infidelity for two years, hoping that it was just a difficult patch. Then she remembers waking up alone one morning after Philip had not come home and thinking, "I'm sick of suffering. I don't want to be hurt anymore, or feel that I am being used as a crutch."

The next day Gilly told Philip the relationship was over. Gilly realized that she no longer felt the need to stay in such a destructive partnership, and that there was a life waiting for her outside the relationship. She took responsibility for the fact that she had put everything second to her rescuing function; as long as she focused on *his* needs, she could avoid examining her own, sometimes overwhelming and frightening, desires for security, love, and acknowledgment. In other words, Gilly had discovered that:

• You must change *yourself*—if you continue to blame your partner you are still caught in the trap.

• Staying in a bad relationship is not "safer" than risking change, or better than being alone, especially if it feeds certain unhealthy, addictive needs.

• Love shouldn't always be painful, which you might think if you have a history of difficult relationships.

Plan of action

To escape the trap, you must have a clear program of action, and stick to it. There may be times when you feel that you are swinging too far in the other direction, but you will probably find that you aren't, you're simply on new ground, so keep going. First, make a list of your needs and your desires. Is your present relationship fulfilling any of these? Learn to express your needs and desires to others in an appropriate way, and so that they are able to meet them. For example, "expecting" someone to know telepathically what you want and to explode with anger when they don't respond in some wildly extravagant way is not appropriate. Address some of the traits that made you fall prey to the relationship in the first place.

• Do what you can to promote your self-esteem. You do not "deserve" a difficult relationship.

• Learn to take responsibility for your life, but realize that you don't have to be perfect.

• Develop reasonable "boundaries" for yourself—and respect other people's. For example, it is perfectly reasonable to say no directly if your partner makes sexual advances and expect that your wish should be respected. Anyone who ignores your clear boundary does so because he or she can't recognize his or her own. Don't build walls, however; you want to protect yourself, not shut yourself off.

• Look at yourself and think about what has made you who you are. For example, if you weren't allowed to express any weakness during childhood, then you may automatically be drawn to a caring role where your own needs are ignored.

Your aim in a relationship should be for a healthy *interdependence,* where partners rely on each other in a well-balanced way for mutual comfort and support, but each one also develops an inner strength on which he or she can draw. It is not realistic to look to any relationship to meet all your needs all the time; rather, try to develop a better understanding of how your needs can be met in different ways—not just from your life companion.

SPOT THE SIGNS

Even if you have successfully escaped from one dependent situation, it can be difficult to avoid slipping into another one, believing that, this time, everything will be different. When you realize that you have made the same mistake again, this may drive your sense of self-worth even lower and so continue the cycle. Learn to spot the immediate danger signs quickly. If you have recently started another relationship and answer yes to all or some of the following, you could be heading for trouble.

Does your new partner...

• have an addiction of any sort—drugs, drink, gambling, over-spending?

• expect you to bale them out of any problems—lending money, lying for them, etc?

• already have another relationship?

• always blame other people for everything that goes wrong in their life?

Do you find yourself...

• developing feelings and types of behavior that seem to be more appropriate to looking after a small child than having an equal relationship with a mature adult?

• making excuses for their behavior—to yourself and others?

• Putting yourself last in all kinds of ways?

• Thinking about ways in which you can change them or fantasizing about what it will be like when they have changed?

CHANGING RELATIONSHIPS—MOVING ON

Surviving the break-up of a relationship is one of life's most difficult challenges. Whether you are the one who is leaving or the one who has been left, it can be very hard to envisage a happier future when you are engulfed by an overwhelming sense of loss and waste. It may be some time before you realize that life can be richer and more promising than it looks from inside your unhappiness.

Coping with change

As you move through life, your relationships change and grow as you do. Inevitably, no matter how much hard work you may have put into it, you will sometimes outgrow a relationship, and will have to accept that separation is the only option—a painful but necessary transition period. This doesn't mean that the relationship was a mistake; it may simply mean that it was right at the time, but that those times have changed.

Alison and Sean met at college and seemed like the perfect couple when they married soon after graduation. During the early years, Sean's job supported them as Alison went back to college to gain further qualifications. As the couple slipped into their thirties, Alison's career was just taking off, while Sean became eager for a family. Alison agreed at first, although eventually she had to admit that she did not at that time, if ever, wish to interrupt her career to raise children. They couldn't reach a compromise and decided to part.

Despite bitterness at the time, when they spoke about their relationship three years later, they remembered what had been good in the marriage and were grateful for the insights the experience had given them into their desires for the future: Sean knew he didn't want to miss out on the experience of fathering, and Alison felt the need for a career and independence.

Living with loss

Separation usually brings great pain. Although it is often thought that it is the abandoned partner who suffers most, this is not necessarily the case, even if the parting is acrimonious. If there was anything

Diving in head first
If a long-term relationship has ended, you will be forced to test new waters in your life. You will only be able to dive in head first and make the most of new possibilities if you let go of the past.

good about the relationship, its demise is bound to affect both partners. Whoever leaves may also experience a burden of guilt for breaking up the partnership, especially if there are children involved.

Many people coping with a break-up fail to realize that they are actually going through a perfectly natural grieving process. Although no physical death has occurred, separation from a partner is still a form of bereavement. If you acknowledge this, and treat yourself gently and patiently as you recover, you will come to accept that the pain will pass and, armed with this greater self-knowledge, you will enjoy life and relationships once more. If you bury your grief, this acceptance will be much harder to reach.

One common reaction is to see a break-up as a blight over everything that has gone before, destroying the memory of anything that was beneficial. Think of your life as an unfolding experience and your relationships as part of that. Your contributions to a partnership—such as your ability to relate affectionately to another human being—are not simply attached to the lost person and therefore gone forever; they never leave you.

The pattern of recovery for both partners can be erratic. During the early months following a break-up, friends may be surprised at how well one or both ex-partners are doing—they rediscover their fun-loving side and look great. However, this is usually just a defence strategy that keeps the person buoyant for a while and wards off the full force of what has happened. Letting off steam is natural while you find your feet, as long as it is not stopping you from getting on with your life.

Talking it through

Never fall into the trap of thinking that no one can possibly appreciate what you are going through. Talking to friends and family can really help to sort out your feelings, and you will be surprised just how much most people will understand. Even when there is little anyone can do in a practical sense, just having someone who will listen to you can be beneficial. Beware, however, of confiding in a new love—it may be unwise to expect him or her to listen to all the details of your story. You could become over-dependent on your new partner, and it is perhaps unfair on both of you to start out in the shadow of an old relationship.

If you feel that the split has thrown up a specific issue that needs objective, specialist help—for example sexual problems, or a tendency to get caught up in abusive relationships—then you may gain a great deal from consulting a counselor.

NEW BEGINNINGS

Anyone who has been through a serious relationship break-up will be anxious about being isolated. Old friendships can be one of the casualties of a break-up, but there are positive sides to the change:
• This is simply a period of readjustment until you find a way of developing new friendships, which you will once the initial shock has worn off.
• Although it can be difficult to know how to start rebuilding your life and making new contacts, you probably know more people than you think and have simply let friendships flag. So get back in contact—making the first move will make you feel in control, too.
• Outside a relationship, good friends come into their own in a way that they simply do not when you have a partner.
• You will be amazed how many of the people you know are going through the same thing.

It's important to realize the value of a supportive network when you are building your new life. Just knowing that there are other people around with whom you can share experiences can make all the difference. Why not be the one to bring a few of these people together? Enquiries among people you know and advertising in the local paper should be enough. Rather than a mournful gathering, support groups can provide entertainment, new friends, and a boost to morale.

Into the blue
Heading off into less troubled waters, to begin your new life, will be much easier if you let yourself be supported by those around you.

Do You Like Where You Live?

What does home mean to you? Is it a place in which you can relax and unwind, a castle whose drawbridge you can pull up and hide from the world, a place of privacy and comfort? Or is it a trap, a source of irritation and stress, and a drain on your energies? The clichéd images of home sweet home are very familiar, but for many the place where they live falls short of this ideal.

Your home is an expression of your personality, and it is important that you are happy there in order to feel in control of your life. Use these pages to examine whether your home makes you feel empowered or powerless, and discover what your home may reveal about you.

Comfort zone

When you were a baby, your home was in the arms of people who loved you. This was the place where you felt most safe. As an adult, you continue to equate home with a place of safety so that, when you feel unsafe, unhappy, and vulnerable, you often turn these feelings outside yourself and express them as a dissatisfaction with your present home. Perhaps, in such instances, you are subconsciously measuring your actual home against the ideal, perfect one of your babyhood.

The following questions will help you to analyze your perfect home:

• Whose house did you most enjoy being in as a child? What did you most like about it?

• Did you move house often as a child?

• Did you suffer a traumatic loss as a child, and move house as a consequence?

• How does your present home compare with your ideal home?

• What, if anything, bothers you about the home you occupy at the moment?

• What do you really want from a home? Don't try to analyze this too much, just write whatever comes into your head.

A moving experience

Do you yearn to uproot everything and go and live in your dream location? Such wishes may stem from ideas about the home that you formed in childhood.

Now look at where you actually live. How does it measure up against your recollections of home as a child? How realistic are your memories, and how much are they idealizations of what you believe to have been a better time and place? A vague but nagging sense of things not being what they should may motivate people to search for their perfect home—a home that can only exist in the mind, not in the real world.

Inside out

How you choose to furnish and decorate your home often reveals something of yourself to the world in general. Many people welcome this opportunity to express their individuality, they enjoy using the home to reflect in a conscious, well-thought-out way their tastes, ideas, and values. However, sometimes the home may expose more about yourself than you care to admit. For example, people who are feeling low or depressed often let things go—an extremely untidy, neglected home suggests an unhappy owner. Do you know someone who has never fully unpacked after a move, many of his or her belongings staying in boxes and bags? The message here is "ready to go."

This person may have difficulties committing him- or herself, and this may be reflected in other areas of his or her life. Another way you may express feelings of insecurity is to surround yourself with the things you liked during your childhood, or that have certain childlike associations, such as lots of teddy bears and soft toys, or fun, novelty items.

Making changes

So, before you blame your home or its location for your general feelings of dissatisfaction or unhappiness, check that your discontent doesn't in fact lie elsewhere—perhaps with an awkward relationship, troublesome family problems, or difficulties at work. Ask yourself what you can do to improve things in these areas.

On a more practical level, however, perhaps there are things about your home you don't like. Some of the changes that people have found effective in turning round a less-than-ideal home situation include: redecorating and tidying up, rearranging the furniture, and making something of the garden, if there is one. If you are living on your own, you may want to consider taking a lodger, or asking a friend to move in with you.

TRADING PLACES

There may come a time when moving house is the most sensible option. People move for many different reasons, some purely practical: they get married, or move in with their partner, their lease runs out, they start a family and need more space, they separate from their partner, their children leave home, and so on. Other reasons may be emotional—wanting to move to somewhere that is less isolated and lonely, or moving away from painful memories, for example. Whatever the reason, moving home rates highly on the stress scale—giving up the familiar for the unknown can be frightening. Make your plans carefully, taking time to consider what you want. You may not find your ideal home, but you should be able to find somewhere with which you can be happy. The following practical guidelines may help:

• Make a list of the essential facilities you need, e.g. shops, public transport or parking, doctor, school. This will help focus your choice.
• Visit different areas you think you might like to live in—not just in bright weather, but also at night, and when it is raining.
• When you have chosen an area ask yourself why it appeals to you, and weigh up the pros and cons: a secluded location may be lonely, your friend who lives in the same area may move, your family who are close by may not give you a moment's peace.
• Consider whether you want a property that will last a lifetime, or something short-term.
• Take a cold look at your financial situation, and seek sound financial advice to determine how much you can afford to spend.

GROWING IN WISDOM

Many people regret each passing year, as if age were taking something from them rather than adding to them. If this represents how you feel about the process of growing older, you could be missing out on a great deal of rewarding personal challenge and fulfillment. Indeed, the time from our maturing as adults, usually considered by psychologists to be in our mid-30s, right up to the end of our old age, is a period of continuous development.

In other words, the tide of our lives doesn't turn when we mature—it keeps coming in. The challenges, choices, and responsibilities we face keep changing. An issue that exercised us in our 30s, for example, is no longer relevant to us in our 70s, and in its place come new concerns. Keeping abreast of them is a dynamic and creative process.

Reconsidering adulthood

Until the middle of the nineteenth century the average life expectancy for women was 40 to 45 years, and for men 45 to 50 years. Many people died much younger than this because of illness, disease,

and childbirth. At the end of the nineteenth century no more than 8 percent of the population survived the age of 60. Today, men are expected to live into their 70s, and women into their 80s. Our experience of adulthood—particularly later adulthood—at the end of the twentieth century is therefore very different. Indeed, a stage of life after parenthood is a fairly new phenomenon in the history of the human race.

Psychologists studying the aging process have split adulthood into three phases, each one leading to the next in a process of growth. Early adulthood, from age 30 to 45, is a period of becoming an individual and establishing a nuclear family and firm friendships. This is when we start to come to terms with ourselves, and to assess our life—what we have done, and what we would still like to do.

The middle phase of adulthood, from age 45 to 60, represents an era of stability, as children are growing up and becoming individuals. This can be a very productive time, when some of a person's best work can be accomplished.

In the so-called Third Age, from age 60, people can look forward to up to 30 years of productive life after their children reach adulthood. This is a time when a person can take a fresh look at his or her life and explore areas that remain unfulfilled.

Welcoming the Third Age

The assumption that old age means inevitable physical and mental decline is incorrect. In fact, scientists have provided proof that growing older can actually enhance mental powers. It is a period that can bring wisdom, peace, and grace.

To make the most of the Third Age—to grow in wisdom rather than let life close in around you—requires a willingness to tackle challenges, and to welcome change and new experiences. In other words, it means pursuing a dynamic, creative life, retaining a thirst for knowledge, and exploration of the world and of the individual within.

Incoming tide
After you reach maturity, your life does not begin inexorably to ebb from you. Growing older gives opportunities for continuous, creative development.

DYNAMIC AGEING

How age affects you is largely up to you. You can imagine yourself years from now sitting, inert, in an armchair for the rest of your life. Or you can visualize a dynamic old age, in which you are busy and feel stretched and rewarded. However, imagining a picture doesn't bring it about: you need to prepare for it. Define goals for yourself. For example, after retirement, you may want to continue your life work in some way, perhaps by writing a book; or you may want to branch out and try something new.

The contemporary English novelist, Mary Wesley, wrote her first novel at age 70. More followed, and several have been televised to great popular acclaim. Teiichi Igarashi was 89 when he first climbed to the top of Japan's Mt Fuji. He repeated this feat annually and became the first ever 100-year-old to conquer the summit.

Planning for the positive

If you want to look ahead to a time when your life changes—through retirement or children leaving home, for example—start finding out now about new opportunities. You have the power to be who you want to be.
• Education, training, and information are crucial in enriching people's lives. Many educational establishments welcome older students.
• Keep redefining your goals and making new ones. Don't dwell on unrealized goals from your younger days.
• Expect to be active. Don't book yourself into the retirement home while you are still healthy.
• Keep levels of stimulation high. Don't imagine that you will be content to potter in the garden if your work has always been important to you.

GETTING HELP

M any people suffer under the tyranny of addictions without realizing that they can seek help. Different addictions and disorders cause particular problems, so it is important to find the right sort of help for the addiction. Some addictions can be successfully dealt with in just a few weeks, while others require a long-term commitment to change. The following organizations and charities can help you find the most effective treatment for any particular problem.

Smoking

Nicotine replacement patches, nicotine gum: available from pharmacists.
Alternative therapies: acupuncture and acupressure; hypnotherapy (see page opposite).
Quit Pack available from Victory House, 170 Tottenham Court Road, London W1P 0HA. Tel. 0171-388 5775.
Counselling line tel. 0171-487 3000.
Full Stop Course, PO Box 2484, London N6 5UX.
An effective course that takes a psychological approach to stopping smoking (75 percent of smokers who take the course are still ex-smokers a year later).

Drug abuse

ADFAM National, 5th floor, Epworth House, 25 City Road, London EC1Y 1AA. Tel. 0171-638 3700
Narcotics Anonymous, UK Service Office, PO Box 1980, London N19 3LS. For general information tel. 0171-272 9040; helpline tel. 0171-730 0009.
Release, 388 Old Street, London EC1V 9LT. Tel. 0171-729 9904.
SCODA (Standing Conference on Drug Abuse). For more information tel. 0171-928 9500.

Alcohol

Alcohol Concern, Waterbridge House, 32-36 Loman Street, London SE1 0EE. Tel. 0171-928 7377.
National network of local councils and advice centers.
Alcoholics Anonymous (AA), General Service Office, PO Box 1, Stonebow House, Stonebow, York Y01 2NJ. Helpline tel. 0171-352 3001.
Al-Anon and Alateen Family Groups, 61 Great Dover Street, London SE1 4YF. Tel. 0171-928 7377.
National Association for Children of Alcoholics, PO Box 64, Fishponds, Bristol BS16 2UH. Tel. 0117 9573432 and 00800 289061.

Addictions, general

ACCEPT (Addictions Community Centres for Education, Prevention and Treatment), 724 Fulham Road, London SW6 5SE. Tel. 0171-371 7477.
APA Community Drug and Alcohol Iniatives, 67-69 Cowcross Street, London EC1M 6BP. Tel. 0171-251 5860.
St Joseph's Centre for Addiction, Holy Cross Hospital, Hindhead Road, Haslemere, Surrey GU27 1NQ. Tel. 01428 656517.

Relationships

(e.g. sex addiction, love addictions, etc. For general counseling and psychotherapy see page opposite)
British Association for Sexual and Marital Therapy, PO Box 62, Sheffield S10 3TS.
Offers counseling and a structured personal program that helps individuals and couples explore their sexual worries. One hour once a week, with a personal program to work on at home.
CODA (Codependents Anonymous), Ashburnham Community Centre, Tetcott Road, London SW10 0SH. Tel. 0171-376 8191.
RELATE, Herbert Gray College, Little Church Street, Rugby, Warwickshire CV21 3AP. Tel. 01788 573241.
Offers help, information, research, and education in all kinds of couple relationships.
Sex and Love Addicts Anonymous, The Augustine Fellowship, PO Box 2040, London W12. Tel. 0171-402 7278.

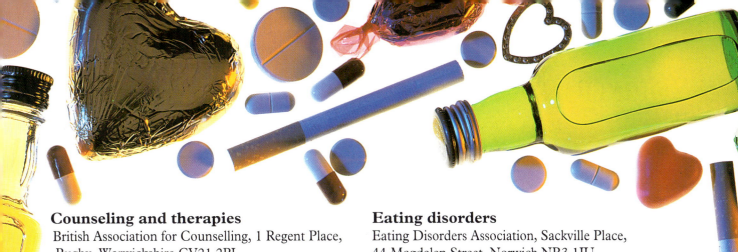

Counseling and therapies

British Association for Counselling, 1 Regent Place, Rugby, Warwickshire CV21 2PJ.
Tel. 01788 578328.

Holds a national directory of counseling organizations. In counseling, individuals are asked to attend once a week for an hour each time, over a variable period of time, usually less than a year. They will be encouraged to explore the problems behind the addiction, and use personal understanding to make appropriate changes.

British Association of Psychotherapists, 37 Mapesbury Road, London NW2 4HJ.
Tel. 0181-452 9823.

Holds a national directory of psychotherapists. In psychotherapy, clients attend sessions regularly, sometimes several times a week for an hour each time. Therapy is usually long term (more than a year), and aims to explore the unconscious motives behind problems.

FOCUS (Forum for Occupational Counselling and Unemployment Services Ltd), Northside House, Mount Pleasant, Hertfordshire EN4 9EB.
Tel. 0181-441 9300.

A national organization that offers counseling and advice on work-related issues such as redundancy, career change, and retirement.

MIND (National Association for Mental Health), Granta House, 15-19 The Broadway, London E15 4BQ. Tel. 0181-519 2122.

A national charity that provides support to people in mental distress. General advice also available over the telephone or by post.

Families

Families Anonymous, The Doddington and Rollo Community Association, Charlotte Despard Avenue, London SW11 5JE. Tel. 0171-498 4680.
Institute of Family Therapy, 43 New Cavendish Street, London W1M 7RG. Tel. 0171-935 1651.
Parent Network, 44-46 Caversham Road, London NW5 2DS. Tel. 0171-485 8535.
Offers courses and workshops on effective parenting.

Eating disorders

Eating Disorders Association, Sackville Place, 44 Magdalen Street, Norwich NR3 1JU.
Tel. 01603 621414. Youth helpline tel. 01603-765 050. between 4.00 pm and 6.00 pm.
The Maisner Centre for Eating Disorders, PO Box 464, Hove, East Sussex BN3 3UG. Tel. 01273 729818.

Stress related problems

The Mental Health Foundation, 37 Mortimer Street, London W1N 7RJ. Tel. 0171-580 0145.
Relaxation for Living Trust, 12 New Street, Chipping Norton, Oxon OX7 5LF. Tel. 01608-646100.
Stressbusters, 48 Camden Street, London NW1 0DX. Tel. 0171-383 7943.

Autogenic training

British Association for Autogenic Training, The Positive Health Centre, 101 Harley Street, London W1N 1DF.
Tel. 0171-935 1811.
Autogenic training is a method of relaxation using a formula of relaxation.

Alternative health organizations
Acupuncture

British Acupuncture Association and Register Ltd, 34 Alderney Street, London SW1V 4EU.
Tel. 0171-834 1012.
British Acupuncture Council, 206 Latimer Road, London W10 6RE. Tel. 0181-964 0222.

Hypnotherapy

British Society of Clinical Hypnotherapists, 229a Sussex Gardens, London W2 2RL. Tel. 0171-402 9037.
Holds national register of qualified practitioners.

Yoga

The Yoga for Health Foundation, Ickwell Bury, Icwell Green, Biggleswade, Bedfordshire SG18 9EF.
Tel. 01767 627271.

SOLUTIONS

Pages 14-15
Check Your Attitudes

1. a=4 b=1 c=2 d=3
2. a=4 b=3 c=1 d=2
3. a=4 b=1 c=3 d=2
4. a=2 b=3 c=4 d=1
5. a=3 b=4 c=1 d=2
6. a=1 b=2 c=3 d=4
7. a=1 b=2 c=3 d=4
8. a=1 b=4 c=3 d=2
9. a=1 b=2 c=3 d=4
10. a=4 b=3 c=2 d=1

Check your answers against the table above, and add up the number of **1s, 2s, 3s** and **4s.**

If you scored one for most questions, it indicates that you tend toward non-assertive responses. Because of your lack of confidence in yourself, you may find it difficult to take decisions and feel responsible for your actions.

If you scored mostly twos, this may indicate that you tend to deal with difficulties by manipulation and by avoiding direct confrontation. It may also show an unwillingness to put yourself in a position where you may be rejected.

Scoring mostly threes suggests that you see many situations as competitive and confrontational, and that your way of dealing with them is to go on the attack—for you, winning is the most important thing of all.

Scoring mainly fours demonstrates a genuine respect both for yourself and for others. You don't feel guilty and you don't need to make other people feel guilty or intimidated. Your self-esteem allows you to take full responsibility for your actions and choices without the need for the approval of others.

Most people will combine various aspects of these personalities in different situations and at different times. The important thing is not to judge or label your behavior, but to pay attention to how you react and what processes are going on inside you.

Page 27
Stress Awareness

The quiz on page 27 is drawn from the "life-events scale" chart created by psychiatrists Thomas Holmes and Richard Rahe (*Journal of Psychosomatic Research*, 1967). By applying a scale of values to a range of significant life events that have taken place within a given year, and then adding them together, the amount of stress you may be experiencing is indicated. If the same event occurred more than once within a year, each time is treated as a separate unit—for example, if you have changed jobs twice in one year, double the score.

Critics of the system have pointed out that the values do not take into account individual responses to stress—in other words, we do not all react to stress in the same way, and what may seem very stressful to one person may well be a minor discomfort to another. The type of stress experienced is also significant. If you've married (50), changed jobs (36), and moved house (25)—all of which you are happy about—then you are unlikely to find these experiences as stressful as, say, elderly relatives moving in (39), major changes at work (29), and the death of a close friend (37), even though both totals would be about the same. This should be taken into account in the analyses below.

1-100: Your life seems to be on a fairly even keel at present, and you are experiencing an acceptable—even necessary—level of stress. However, such an assessment may not give an accurate picture if you have scored 73 for a divorce, or 65 for separation. If you scored with a single high-value life event that you find traumatic, then you may well be experiencing more stress than your score suggests.

101-200: You are experiencing a moderate amount of stress. How you cope with it, and how it affects you, depends on how well you deal with stress generally, and the kind of stress you are experiencing. However, your health may need watching. Are you eating a well-balanced diet? Try to take some regular exercise, if you are not already, and build in some enjoyable periods of relaxation.

201–300: You are experiencing a high degree of stress. Depending on your character type and how well you handle stress, your health may need careful monitoring. Also look at how you may be contributing to the stress. What measures can you take to minimize the amount of distress you are experiencing? Are you taking on too much, for example? Read through the text on page 26, and also see pages 104–105 "The Secret of Empowerment" and pages 112–114 "Are You Assertive?" Make sure you are eating properly, take some regular exercise, and try to make sure you get rest and leisure time.

Pages 94–5.
Are You Stuck on Love?

When you have added up your score, read the analysis that applies to you.

0–35 points You have experienced some of the situations described with one or even a few partners, but they do not define a pattern in your love life. You're not a love addict. You may sometimes find yourself doing things that suggest you may not be in a healthy relationship: for example, making excuses when your partner continually puts you down in public, or phoning them when they say they are working late to make sure they are there. But you

probably have a good idea of what makes a successful relationship and are able to choose healthy partners and put this knowledge into practice.

36–70 points You have found yourself in some of the situations described with a number of partners. Perhaps you find that a few of your past relationships have run along the lines of the scenarios described, while other relationships have shown up only one or two symptoms. Look carefully at any patterns that you see developing in your love life and try to understand what it is that drives you to run your relationships along these lines. You are not a love addict—but could become one.

71–102 points You find yourself living out the same pattern over and over again with nearly every partner. Perhaps this is the first time you have realized it. If so, you have already made great strides forward. The challenge ahead of you is not to ignore this knowledge, but to tackle the issues that compel you to conduct your love life in this way. You may, however, have been aware of this pattern for some time, but have chosen to ignore it or have been afraid of working to change it. Re-read the box on "Healthy Relationships" (page 93) and look in the bibliography for useful books. You may also want to consider some form of counseling, therapy, or group work.

Your partner Now look at which questions applied to your present or last partner if you are currently alone. This is an especially useful exercise if your own score is high. If you discover that your partner's score is also high, this is not unusual—love addicts often choose other love addicts with whom to have a relationship. The woman who discovers that every lover she has cheats on her is unwittingly choosing "love 'em and leave 'em" Casanovas. The seducer who makes conquests with his insistent charisma and passion will choose vulnerable women who are likely to fall for his line. Once the choice of a partner is made, the relationship will follow a more or less predictable course.

The woman who can't leave her man even though he abuses her stays because she believes that he needs her, that he will change, that he will crumble without her. She chooses life's victims who are also aggressors. Love addicts stuck in the first phase of love, on the other hand, choose people who ignite a sexual spark. Once this has been extinguished, the addict must move on.

Remember, it takes both partners to make a love addicted relationship. Examining how your relationships work (who plays which role) will help you to see the pattern and break free.

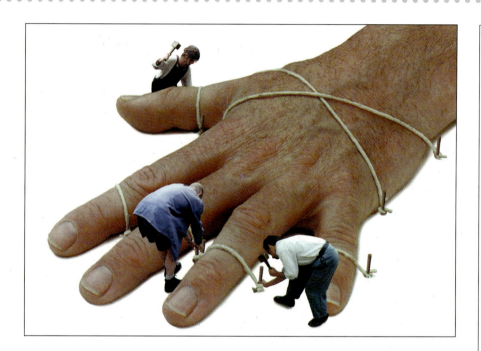

Pages 106-107 Do You Feel Powerless?

Relationships and social life
Scoring mainly ones and twos in these categories suggests that the issues causing you to feel most powerless are usually emotional ones. You tend to undervalue yourself and your own opinions, and fear rejection or disapproval if you speak out.

Work and daily life
Consistently low scores in these areas could indicate a distorted view of those in authority. If this is the case, your feelings of powerlessness may stem from a flawed assumption that some people are totally competent and in control, and therefore can never be questioned or challenged. (See "Can You Cope with Authority" on pp. 54-55.)

The world
Scoring mainly ones and twos in this category suggests that you feel impotent when it comes to the important issues facing mankind. This paralyzing negativity could be preventing you from contributing in small but important ways such as campaigning for change, or raising or contributing funds on behalf of a pressure group.

If you scored highly in every category, you have a healthy grasp of your own ability to exert control in appropriate ways. As a result, you are probably optimistic and action-driven. If your score was consistently low, addressing your feelings of helplessness and attempting to change them will help lift the fears that limit your success. Reading through the rest of the chapter will give you some ideas of how you might go about this; see also pages 12-19 and 28-39 in Chapter One.

Pages 120-121
Different Styles

Man in suit
A man in a well-made, conventional suit signals status, respectability, and success. It would be easy to assume from his appearance that he is a well-established businessman. However, consider the following alternatives: He is unemployed and on his way to an important job interview; he is a self-employed craftsman who has borrowed a suit from a friend for an interview with the bank manager for a loan; he is on his way to a formal function in which a suit is required wear.
Picture match: the smart car.

Woman in trouser suit
A mature woman in a stylish trouser suit suggests someone who values both style and comfort. Her whole appearance and demeanour indicates a strong self-respect, and an awareness of a certain status and responsibility in life. This woman could be anything: a doctor in a general practice; a solicitor; someone who works in the media, such as a writer, editor, or journalist; a lecturer; an architect. She might also be a full-time wife, where her role is an active one as skilful hostess in charge of a busy household.
Picture match: medical equipment.

Young woman in dress

A young woman who likes to dress fashionably, but veers toward artistic expression rather than a straight high-street fashion look. She enjoys experimenting with different styles, and is clearly at ease with her feminity. She may be at college studying art or fashion design; a hairdresser; a beautician; or a makeup stylist.

Picture match: the makeup.

Woman in casual wear

Here is someone dressed for ease and convenience, a busy mother, perhaps. She may also be someone who works from home, and therefore dresses to please herself. Like the other people in the gallery, however, her appearance may be deceptive; a day off from work may see a busy executive relaxing in casual style.

Picture match: the basket of shopping.

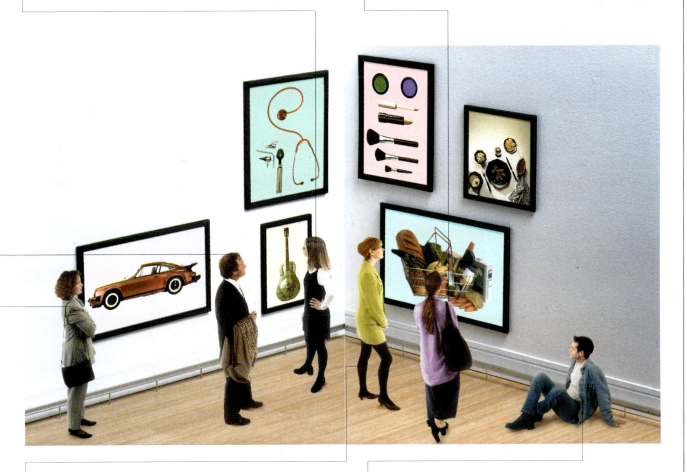

Woman in suit

This young woman exudes confidence and success. She's not dressed conventionally enough for a job in banking or commerce, but she could be a successful sales executive, or possibly climbing the corporate ladder in a large firm. She could also run her own business. She may have cosmopolitan tastes.

Picture match: the Japanese dishes.

Young man in casual wear

The jeans "uniform" appeals to a wide spectrum of society. The young man could be a student, social worker, plumber, electrician, graphic designer, unemployed—or even a rock star in the making. His image identifies him as belonging to a recognized strand of today's youth culture.

Picture match: the guitar.

INDEX

BIBLIOGRAPHY

Richard Nelson Bolles, *What Color is Your Parachute?: A Practical Manual for Job-Hunters and Career-Changers*; Ten Speed Press, California, U.S., updated yearly.

Julia Buckroyd, *Eating Your Heart Out: The Emotional Meaning of Eating Disorders*; Optima, London, U.K., 1989.

Chérie Carter-Scott, *Negaholics: Overcome Your Lack of Confidence and Live the Life You Really Want To*; Century, London, U.K., 1990.

Stephen R. Covey, *The 7 Habits of Highly Effective People*; Fireside, New York, U.S., 1989.

Dr. Windy Dryden & Jack Gordon, *Beating the Comfort Trap*; Sheldon Press, London, U.K., 1993.

Diane Fassel, *Working Ourselves to Death: The High Cost of Workaholism and the Rewards of Recovery*; Thorsons, London, U.K., 1992.

Thomas A. Harris, MD, *I'm OK—You're OK*; Pan Books Ltd, London, U.K., 1973.

Muriel James and Dorothy Jongeward, *Born to Win*; Addison-Wesley, Reading, Massachusetts, U.S., 1994.

Susan Jeffers, *Feel the Fear and Do It Anyway*; Arrow Books Limited, London, U.K., 1991.

Charlotte Davis Kasl, *Women, Sex and Addiction*; Mandarin, London, U.K., 1990.

Antony Kidman, *Tactics for Changing Your Life*; Kogan Page Limited, London, U.K., 1986.

Pia Mellody, with Andrea Wells Miller and J. Keith Miller, *Facing Codependence*; HarperCollins, New York, U.S., 1989.

Pia Mellody, with Andrea Wells Miller and J. K. Miller, *Facing Love Addiction*; HarperCollins, New York, U.S., 1992.

Joseph O'Connor and John Seymour, *Introducing Neuro-Linguistic Programming*; Aquarian Press, London, U.K., 1993.

Gillian Riley, *How to Stop Smoking and Stay Stopped for Good*; Vermilion, London, U.K., 1992.

Anthony Robbins, *Awaken the Giant Within: How to Take Control of Your Mental, Emotional, Physical and Financial Destiny*; Simon & Schuster Ltd, London, U.K., 1993.

Anthony Robbins, *Unlimited Power*; Simon & Schuster Ltd, London, U.K., 1988

Dr. Judith Rodin, *Body Traps: How to Overcome Your Body Obsessions—and Liberate the Real You*; Vermilion, London, U.K., 1992.

Corinne Sweet, *Off The Hook: How to Break Free from Addiction and Enjoy a New Way of Life*; Judy Piatkus (Publishers) Ltd, London, U.K., 1994.

Anni Townend, *Developing Assertiveness*; Routledge, London, U.K., 1991.

Peter Trachtenberg, *The Casanova Complex: Compulsive Lovers and Their Women*; Eden Paperbacks, London, U.K., 1989.

Murray Watts & Professor Cary L. Cooper, *Relax: Dealing with Stress*; BBC Books, London, U.K., 1992

CREDITS
Illustrators
Gail Armstrong, Maria Beddoes, Colour Company, Debut Art (agent), Roy Flooks, Steve Rawlings, Martyn Ridgewell, Private View (agent)

Modelmakers
Atlas Models, Peter Griffiths, Mark Jamieson, Mark Reddy, Mike Shepherd, Justin Wilson

Photographers
Michel Focard de Fontefiguiéres, Mark Hamilton, Stuart Haygarth, Romy O'Driscoll, Neil Phillips, Mark Preston, Jonny Thompson, Andy White, Alex Wilson

Picture Sources

The publishers are grateful to the following picture libraries for permission to reproduce their photographs:
Action Plus 84; **Bruce Coleman Ltd** *Dr Stephen Coyne* 132 (center); **Pictures Colour Library** 75, 114 (top right); **Pictor International** 22-23; **Tony Stone Images** *Bruce Ayers* 95 (bottom right), *Ed Pritchard* 26 (top), *John Waterman* 93 (bottom right); **Zefa** 94 (bottom right), *Kotoh* 94 (bottom left), *Pfander* 115 (bottom)

Every effort has been made to trace copyright holders. If there are any unintentional omissions, we would be pleased to insert appropriate acknowledgments in any subsequent editions of this publication.